Literaturhinweise

Kelten:

Barry Cunliffe, Die Kelten und ihre Geschichte, Bergisch Gladbach 1980.

Gerhard Dobesch, Die Kelten in Österreich nach den ältesten Berichten der Antike. Das norische Königreich und seine Beziehungen zu Rom im 2. Jahrhundert v. Chr., Wien - Köln - Graz 1980.

P. M. Duval, Die Kelten. Universum der Kunst 25, München 1978.

Jan Filip, Keltové ve středni Evrope, Praha 1956.

Jan Filip, Die keltische Zivilisation und ihr Erbe, Prag 1961.

Robert Göbl, Typologie und Chronologie der keltischen Münzprägung in Noricum, Veröffentlichungen der Kommission für Numismatik der österr. Akademie der Wissenschaften, Band 2, Wien 1973.

J. V. Megaw, Art of the European Iron Age. A Study of the Elusive Image, Bath o. J. (1970).

Richard Pittioni. Urzeit, von etwa 80 000 bis 15 v. Chr. Geb., in: Geschichte Österreichs, Band I, Wien 1980.

Die Kelten in Mitteleuropa. Kultur – Kunst – Wirtschaft, Katalog der Salzburger Landesausstellung Hallein, Salzburg 1980.

Symposium Ausklang der Latène Zivilisation und Anfänge der germanischen Besiedlung im mittleren Donaugebiet, Bratislava 1927.

Römer:

Manfred Kandler, Hermann Vetters, Der römische Limes in Österreich. Ein Führer, Wien 1986.

Títus Kolník, Römische und germanische Kunst in der Slowakei, Bratislava 1984.

A. Lengyel, G. T. B. Radan, The Archaeology of Roman Pannonia, Budapest 1980.

Gertrud Pascher, Römische Siedlungen und Straßen im Limesgebiet zwischen Enns und Leitha. Der römische Limes in Österreich, Heft XIX, Wien 1949.

Sándor Soproni, Die letzten Jahrzehnte des pannonischen Limes, Münchner Beiträge zur Vor- und Frühgeschichte, Band 38, München 1985.

Herma Stiglitz, Manfred Kandler, Werner Jobst, Carnuntum, in: Aufstieg und Niedergang der römischen Welt, Geschichte und Kultur Roms im Spiegel der neuen Forschung II, 6, Berlin 1977.

Vindobona – die Römer im Wiener Raum, Katalog der 52. Sonderausstellung des Historischen Museums der Stadt Wien, Karlsplatz, Wien 1978.

Die Römer an der Donau. Noricum und Pannonien, Katalog der Landesausstellung Schloß Traun, Petronell, NÖ, 1973.

Berichte über römische Bauten in Mähren und der Slowakei, herausgegeben anläßlich des 14. Internationalen Limeskongresses 1986, Archeologické rozhledy XXXVIII-1986. 4, Praha 1986.

Germanen:

Marianne Pollak, Die germanischen Bodenfunde des 1.–4. Jahrhunderts n. Chr. im nördlichen Niederösterreich, Studien zur Ur- und Frühgeschichte des Donau- und Ostalpenraumes, Band I, Wien 1980.

Helmut Windl, Niederösterreich nördlich der Donau in der römischen Periode, Wissenschaftliche Schriftenreihe Niederösterreich, Band 52, 1981.

Die Germanen. Geschichte und Kultur der germanischen Stämme in Mitteleuropa. Ein Handbuch in zwei Bänden, Berlin 1976 und 1983.

Germanen, Awaren, Slawen in Niederösterreich, Katalog des Nö. Landesmuseums N.F. 75, 1977.

Völkerwanderungszeit:

István Bóna, Der Anbruch des Mittelalters, Gepiden und Langobarden im Karpatenbecken, Budapest 1976.

Eugippius, Das Leben des Heiligen Severin (lateinisch-deutsch), Einführung, Übersetzung und Erläuterung von Rudolf Noll, Passau 1981.

Herwig Friesinger, Horst Adler, Die Zeit der Völkerwanderung in Niederösterreich, Wissenschaftliche Schriftenreihe Niederösterreich, Band 41/42, 1979.

Otto J. Maenchen-Helfen, Die Welt der Hunnen, eine Analyse ihrer historischen Dimension, Wien 1978.

Wilfried Menghin, Die Langobarden, Archäologie und Geschichte, Stuttgart 1985.

Herbert Mitscha-Märheim, Dunkler Jahrhunderte goldene Spuren. Die Völkerwanderungszeit in Österreich, Wien 1963.

Rudolf Noll, Frühes Christentum in Österreich, Wien 1954.

Helmut Roth, Kunst der Völkerwanderungszeit, Propyläen Kunstgeschichte, Supplementband IV, 1979.

Helmut Roth, Kunst und Handwerk im frühen Mittelalter, Archäologische Zeugnisse von Childerich I. bis zu Karl dem Großen, Stuttgart 1986.

Ludwig Schmidt, Die Ostgermanen, München 1933.

Bedřich Svoboda, Čechy v době stěhováni narodů, Monumenta Archaeologica, Praha 1965.

Jaroslav Tejral, Grundzüge der Völkerwanderungszeit in Mähren, Studie Archeologického ústavu Československé Akademie věd v Brně, Ročník IV, 2, Praha 1976.

Jaroslav Tejral, Mähren im 5. Jahrhundert. Studie Archeologického ústavu Československé Akademie věd v Brně, 3, Praha 1973.

László Várady, Das letzte Jahrhundert Pannoniens 376–476, Amsterdam 1969.

László Várady, Epochenwechsel um 476, Budapest 1984.

Joachim Werner, Beiträge zur Archäologie des Attila-Reiches, Bayerische Akademie der Wissenschaften, phil.-hist. Klasse, Abhandlungen N. F. Heft 38 A, B, München 1956.

Joachim Werner, Die Langobarden in Pannonien, Beiträge zur Kenntnis der langobardischen Bodenfunde vor 568, Bayerische Akademie der Wissenschaften, phil.-hist. Klasse, Abhandlungen N. F. Heft 55 A, B, München 1962.

Herwig Wolfram, Geschichte der Goten, München 1979.

Erich Zöllner, Geschichte der Franken bis zur Mitte des sechsten Jahrhunderts, München 1970.

Severin zwischen Römerzeit und Völkerwanderung, Katalog der Ausstellung des Landes Oberösterreich im Stadtmuseum Enns 1982.

Die Völker an der mittleren und unteren Donau im 5. und 6. Jahrhundert. Berichte des Symposions der Kommission für Frühmittelalterforschung, 1978, Stift Zwettl, Niederösterreich 1980.

Germanen, Awaren, Slawen in Niederösterreich, Katalog des Nö. Landesmuseums, N.F. 75, 1977.

Bayern – Alamannen:

Rainer Christlein, Die Alamannen, Stuttgart 1978.

Hertha Ladenbauer-Orel, Linz-Zizlau. Das baierische Gräberfeld an der Traunmündung, Wien 1960.

Frauke Stein, Adelsgräber des achten Jahrhunderts in Deutschland. Germanische Denkmäler der Völkerwanderungszeit Serie A, Band IX, Berlin 1967.

Joachim Werner, Das alamannische Fürstengrab von Wittislingen, München 1950.

Die Bayern und ihre Nachbarn, Band I und II, Berichte des Symposions der Kommission für Frühmittelalterforschung 1982, Stift Zwettl, NÖ, Wien 1985.

Baiernzeit in Oberösterreich, Ausstellung des Oö. Landesmuseums, Katalog-Nr. 96, Linz 1977.

Geschichte Salzburgs, Band I (Hg. H. Dopsch), Salzburg 1984.

Awaren:

Alexander Avenarius, Die Awaren in Europa, Bratislava 1974.

Zlata Cilinska, Slawisch-Awarisches Gräberfeld in Nové Zámky, Archaeologica Slovaca-Fontes VII, 1966.

Dezsö Csallany, Archäologische Denkmäler der Awarenzeit in Mitteleuropa. Schrifttum und Fundorte, Budapest 1956.

Falko Daim, Andreas Lippert, Das awarische Gräberfeld von Sommerein am Leithagebirge, NÖ, Studien zur Archäologie der Awaren 1, österr. Akademie der Wissenschaften, phil.-hist. Klasse, Denkschriften 170. Band, Wien 1984.

Falko Daim, Die Awaren in Niederösterreich, Wissenschaftliche Schriftenreihe Niederösterreich, Band 28, 1977.

Falko Daim, Das awarische Gräberfeld von Leobersdorf, NÖ, Studien zur Archäologie der Awaren 3, österr. Akademie der Wissenschaften, phil.-hist. Klasse, Denkschriften XXX, 1987.

Jan Eisner, Devínska Nová Ves, Slovanské pohřebiště, Bratislava 1952.

Eva Garam, Das awarenzeitliche Gräberfeld von Kisköre, Fontes Archaeologici Hungariae 1979.

Ilona Kovrig, Das awarenzeitliche Gräberfeld von Alattyan, Fontes Archaeologici Hungariae S.N. XI, 1963.
Gyula László, István Racz, Der Goldschatz von Nagyszentmiklos, Budapest - Wien - München 1977.
Gyula László, The Art of the Migration Period, University of Miami Press 1974.
Andreas Lippert, Das awarenzeitliche Gräberfeld von Zwölfaxing in Niederösterreich, Prähistorische Forschungen Heft 7, Wien 1969.
Joachim Werner, Der Grabfund von Malaja Pereščepina und Kuvrat, Kagan der Bulgaren, Bayerische Akademie der Wissenschaften, phil.-hist. Klasse, Abhandlungen N.F. Heft 91, München 1984.
Joachim Werner, Der Schatzfund von Vrap in Albanien, Studien zur Archäologie der Awaren 2, österr. Akademie der Wissenschaften, phil.-hist. Klasse, Denkschriften 184. Band, Wien 1986.
Die Bayern und ihre Nachbarn, Band I und II, Berichte des Symposions der Kommission für Frühmittelalterforschung 1982, Stift Zwettl, NÖ, Wien 1985.
Awaren in Europa, Katalog Ausstellung Ungarn, Frankfurt a. Main, Nürnberg 1985.
Germanen, Awaren, Slawen in Niederösterreich, Katalog des Nö. Landesmuseums, N.F. Nr. 75, 1977.

Slawen:

Darina Bialeková, Dávne slovanské kovácstvo, Bratislava 1981.
Bořivoj Dostál, Slovanská pohřebiště ze střední doby hradištné na Moravě, Praha 1966.
Herwig Friesinger, Studien zur Archäologie der Slawen in Niederösterreich I und II, Mitteilungen der prähistorischen Kommission der österr. Akademie der Wissenschaften, XV./XVI. Band 1971–1974 und XVII./XVIII. Band 1975–1977.
Joachim Herrmann (Hg.), Welt der Slawen, Geschichte, Gesellschaft, Kultur, Leipzig 1986.
Josef Poulík, Mikulčice, Praha 1975.
Josef Poulík, Bohuslav Chropovský, Velká Morava a počátky Československé státnosti, Bratislava 1985.
Agnes Cs. Sós, Die slawische Bevölkerung Westungarns im 9. Jahrhundert, München 1973.
Zdeněk Váňa, Einführung in die Frühgeschichte der Slawen, Neumünster 1970.
Herwig Wolfram, Conversio Bagoariorum et Carantanorum, Böhlau Quellenbücher, Graz 1979.
Herwig Wolfram, Die Karolingerzeit in Niederösterreich, Wissenschaftliche Schriftenreihe Niederösterreich, Band 46, 1980.
Germanen, Awaren, Slawen in Niederösterreich, Katalog des Nö. Landesmuseums, N.F. 75, 1977.
1 000 Jahre Babenberger in Österreich, Katalog des Nö. Landesmuseums, N.F. Nr. 66, Wien 1976.
Die Kuenringer. Das Werden des Landes Niederösterreich, Katalog des Nö. Landesmuseums, N.F. Nr. 110, Wien 1981.

Ungarn:

Antal Bartha, Hungarian Society in the 9th and 10th Centuries, Studia Historica Academiae Scientiarum Hungaricae, 85, Budapest 1975.
Istvan Dienes, Die Ungarn und die Zeit der Landnahme, Budapest 1972.
Géza Fehér, Karol Éry, Alán Kralovánszky, A Közép-Duna-Medence magyar honfoglalás – és kora Árpád-kori sírleletei. Leletkataszter (Ungarische landnahme- und frühárpádenzeitliche Grabfunde im Mitteldonaubecken. Fundortverzeichnis) Régészeti Tanulmányok 2, Budapest 1962.
Szabolcs de Vajay, Der Eintritt des ungarischen Stämmebundes in die europäische Geschichte (862–933), Studia Hungarica 4, Mainz 1968.

Regensburg
Passau
Freysing
München
Bayern
Oberöster
Kremsmüns
Chiemsee
Innsbruck

booq
publishing

Editorial project:
2019 © **booq** Publishing, S.L.
c/ Domènech, 7-9, 2º 1ª
08012 Barcelona, Spain
T: +34 93 268 80 88
www.booqpublishing.com

ISBN 978-84-9936-093-5

© Editions du Layeur
Dépôt Légal : 2019
ISBN : 978-2-915126-58-7
Imprimé chez Shenzhen Hua Xin
Colour Printing Co., Ltd. en juillet 2019

Editorial coordinator:
Claudia Martínez Alonso

Art director:
Mireia Casanovas Soley

Editor and layout:
Francesc Zamora Mola

Translation:
booq Publishing, S.L.
[DE] [FR] [ES]

Printing in China

The simple presence of plants in interior spaces provides us with soothing, restorative, and mood-enhancing benefits. This is only achieved when we interact with natural elements using all our senses. Only then, can we experience the physical and psychological benefits of nature. This also comes with the opportunity for a better understanding and appreciation of the natural world. While there is nothing innovative about surrounding ourselves with plants, there is, however, a continuous effort to come up with new forms to strengthen our relationship with nature. Most of these forms focus on the fusion of natural elements and design or artistic concepts. This search opens up a world of exciting indoor gardening possibilities to fill our spaces with greenery.

We have found in terrariums a space-efficient means to connect with nature and a creative way to venture away from the average houseplant display. The creation of terrariums provides us with the opportunity to surround ourselves with plants, in spite of the limitations that come with city living. Urban environments grow increasingly denser, and spaces become increasingly smaller. For small apartment dwellers, terrariums are perhaps the closest to a garden of their own.

Certainly, terrarium design has gone a long ways since Doctor Nathaniel Bagshaw Ward accidentally created a small closed ecosystem in the Victorian era. This discovery, which successfully paved the path for a new means of transporting plants overseas, became a popular design piece that could be enjoyed by urbanites in their homes despite the shortage of space, light, and good air quality.

Creating terrariums and caring for them shows the way to learn the secrets of plants and their natural habitat. These miniature landscapes draw us into the fascinating world of plants and invite us to learn more about them.

When looking at a terrarium up close, we can see an extraordinary world that normally lies at foot level. At first glance, terrariums offer a thoughtful arrangement of small plants, branches and pebbles or sand, but on close inspection, a new dimension is revealed. The micro-environment contained in the terrarium is no less than a tiny replication of an ecosystem in our natural world. The parallel between the two is striking because the similarities are not merely visual, but also functional. Closed terrariums, for instance, recreate the water cycle so important in an ecosystem.

Working at a small scale invites people into a personal relationship with nature and seems to offer the opportunity to create something that is real and unreal at the same time. The creations are both playful and contemplative, sometimes even storytelling. Terrarium narratives unfold all sorts of worlds where imagination has no boundaries.

Schon alleine die Anwesenheit von Pflanzen in Innenräumen bietet uns beruhigende, regenerierende und stimmungsaufhellende Vorteile. Dies wird nurdurch die Interaktion mit natürlichen Elementen und mit allen Sinnen erreicht. Nur so können wir die physischen und psychischen Vorteile der Natur erleben. Dies bietet auch die Möglichkeit zu einem besseren Verständnis der Natur. Es ist zwar nichts Innovatives daran, sich mit Pflanzen zu umgeben. Dennoch gibt es immer wieder Bestrebungen neue Formen zu entwickeln, um unsere Beziehung zur Natur zu stärken. Die meisten dieser Formen konzentrieren sich auf die Verschmelzung natürlicher Elemente mit Design- und/oder künstlerischen Konzepten. Diese Suche eröffnet eine Welt voller aufregender Indoor-Gartenmöglichkeiten, um unsere Räume mit Grün zu füllen.

Mit Terrarien haben wir ein platzsparendes Mittel gefunden, um uns mit der Natur zu verbinden, das gleichzeitig eine kreative Möglichkeit darstellt, sich von der durchschnittlichen Zimmerpflanzenausstellung zu lösen. Die Schaffung von Terrarien bietet uns die Möglichkeit, uns mit Pflanzen zu umgeben. Und das trotz der Einschränkungen, die das Leben in der Stadt mit sich bringt. Die städtische Umgebung wird immer dichter und die Räume immer kleiner. Für Bewohner kleiner Wohnungen sind Terrarien wohl die beste Annäherung an einen eigenen Garten.

Sicherlich hat das Terrariodesign einen langen Weg zurückgelegt, seit Dr. Nathaniel Bagshaw Ward in der viktorianischen Ära versehentlich ein kleines geschlossenes Ökosystem geschaffen hat. Diese Entdeckung, die erfolgreich den Weg für ein neues Transportmittel für Pflanzen nach Übersee ebnete, wurde zu einem beliebten Designobjekt, das die Stadtbewohner trotz Platzmangel, Licht und guter Luftqualität zu Hause genießen konnten.

Die Gestaltung und Pflege von Terrarien zeigt den Weg, die Geheimnisse der Pflanzen und ihren natürlichen Lebensraum zu ergründen. Diese Miniaturlandschaften entführen uns in die faszinierende Welt der Pflanzen und laden uns ein, mehr über sie zu erfahren.

Wenn wir ein Terrarium aus der Nähe betrachten, können wir eine außergewöhnliche Welt sehen, die normalerweise auf Fußhöhe liegt. Auf den ersten Blick bieten Terrarien eine durchdachte Anordnung kleiner Pflanzen, Äste und Kiesel oder Sand. Aber bei genauerer Betrachtung zeigt sich eine neue Dimension. Die im Terrarium enthaltene Mikroumgebung ist nicht weniger als die winzige Replikation eines Ökosystems in der Natur. Die Parallele zwischen beiden ist auffallend, denn die Ähnlichkeiten sind nicht nur visuell, sondern auch funktional. Geschlossene Terrarien zum Beispiel stellen den in einem Ökosystem so wichtigen Wasserkreislauf wieder her.

Die Arbeit im Kleinformat lädt Menschen in eine persönliche Beziehung zur Natur ein und scheint die Möglichkeit zu bieten, etwas Reales und Unwirkliches gleichzeitig zu schaffen. Die Kreationen sind sowohl verspielt als auch kontemplativ, manchmal sogar erzählend. Terrarienerzählungen entfalten alle möglichen Welten, in denen der Fantasie keine Grenzen gesetzt sind.

La simple présence de plantes dans les espaces intérieurs nous procure des bienfaits apaisants, réparateurs et rehausseurs d'humeur. Ceci n'est possible que lorsque nous interagissons avec des éléments naturels en utilisant tous nos sens. Ce n'est qu'alors que nous pourrons expérimenter les bienfaits physiques et psychologiques de la nature. Cela s'accompagne également d'une meilleure compréhension et d'une meilleure appréciation du monde naturel. S'il n'y a rien d'innovant à s'entourer de plantes, il y a cependant un effort continu à effectuer pour trouver de nouvelles formes pour renforcer notre relation avec la nature. La plupart de ces formes se concentrent sur la fusion d'éléments naturels et de concepts de design ou artistiques. Cette recherche ouvre un monde de possibilités passionnantes de jardinage intérieur pour remplir nos espaces de verdure.

Nous avons trouvé dans les terrariums un moyen peu encombrant d'entrer en contact avec la nature et une façon créative de s'éloigner de l'exposition moyenne des plantes d'intérieur. La création de terrariums nous donne l'occasion de nous entourer de plantes, malgré les limites de la vie urbaine. Les environnements urbains deviennent de plus en plus denses et les espaces deviennent de plus en plus petits. Pour les habitants de petits appartements, les terrariums représentent peut-être la façon la plus rapprochante d'avoir d'un jardin à eux.

Certes, la conception des terrariums a fait beaucoup de chemin depuis que le docteur Nathaniel Bagshaw Ward a accidentellement créé un petit écosystème fermé à l'époque victorienne. Cette découverte, qui a ouvert la voie à un nouveau moyen de transport des plantes à l'étranger, est devenue une pièce de design populaire dont les citadins pouvaient profiter à l'intérieur de leurs maisons malgré le manque d'espace, de lumière et de qualité de l'air.

La création de terrariums et leur entretien permettent d'apprendre les secrets des plantes et de leur habitat naturel. Ces paysages miniatures nous entraînent dans le monde fascinant des plantes et nous invitent à en apprendre davantage à leur sujet.

Quand on regarde un terrarium de près, on peut voir un monde extraordinaire qui se trouve normalement au niveau des pieds. Au premier coup d'œil, les terrariums offrent un arrangement réfléchi de petites plantes, de branches et de galets ou de sable, mais, à y regarder de près, une nouvelle dimension se révèle. Le micro-environnement contenu dans le terrarium n'est rien de moins qu'une minuscule réplique d'un écosystème dans notre monde naturel. Le parallèle entre les deux est frappant parce que les similitudes ne sont pas seulement visuelles, mais aussi fonctionnelles. Les terrariums fermés, par exemple, recréent le cycle de l'eau si essentiel dans un écosystème.

Travailler à petite échelle invite les gens à adopter une relation personnelle avec la nature et semble leur offrir l'opportunité de créer quelque chose de réel et d'irréel en même temps. Les créations sont à la fois ludiques et contemplatives, parfois même narratives. Les récits de terrariums dévoilent toutes sortes de mondes où l'imagination n'a pas de frontières.

La simple presencia de plantas en los espacios interiores nos proporciona beneficios calmantes, restauradores y que mejoran el estado de ánimo. Esto solo se logra cuando interactuamos con elementos naturales utilizando todos nuestros sentidos. Solo entonces podremos experimentar los beneficios físicos y psicológicos de la naturaleza. Si bien no hay nada innovador en rodearnos de plantas, sí hay, sin embargo, un esfuerzo continuo para encontrar nuevas formas de fortalecer nuestra relación con la naturaleza. La mayoría de estas formas se centran en la fusión de elementos naturales con conceptos de diseño o artísticos. Esta búsqueda abre un mundo de excitantes posibilidades de jardinería de interior para llenar nuestros espacios de verdor.

Hemos encontrado en los terrarios un medio eficiente en cuanto al espacio para conectarse con la naturaleza y una forma creativa de aventurarse más allá de la simple exhibición de plantas de interior. La creación de terrarios nos da la oportunidad de rodearnos de plantas, a pesar de las limitaciones que conlleva la vida en la ciudad. Los entornos urbanos son cada vez más densos y los espacios cada vez más pequeños. Para los habitantes de apartamentos pequeños, los terrarios son quizás los más cercanos a un jardín propio.

El diseño de terrarios ha recorrido un largo camino desde que el doctor Nathaniel Bagshaw Ward creó accidentalmente un pequeño ecosistema cerrado en la era victoriana. Este descubrimiento, que allanó el camino para un nuevo medio de transporte de plantas al extranjero, se convirtió en una pieza de diseño popular que los urbanitas podían disfrutar en sus hogares a pesar de la escasez de espacio, luz y buena calidad del aire.

Crear terrarios y cuidarlos muestra el camino para aprender los secretos de las plantas y su hábitat natural. Estos paisajes en miniatura nos adentran en el fascinante mundo de las plantas y nos invitan a aprender más sobre ellas.

Cuando observamos de cerca un terrario, podemos ver un mundo extraordinario que normalmente se encuentra al nivel de los pies. A primera vista, los terrarios ofrecen un arreglo reflexivo de pequeñas plantas, ramas y guijarros o arena, pero al examinarlos de cerca, nos revelan una nueva dimensión. El microambiente contenido en el terrario es nada menos que una pequeña réplica de un ecosistema en nuestro mundo natural. El paralelismo entre los dos es sorprendente porque las similitudes no son meramente visuales, sino también funcionales. Los terrarios cerrados, por ejemplo, recrean el ciclo del agua tan importante en un ecosistema.

Trabajar a pequeña escala invita a la gente a una relación personal con la naturaleza y parece ofrecer la oportunidad de crear algo que es real e irreal al mismo tiempo. Las creaciones son a la vez lúdicas y contemplativas, a veces incluso narrativas. Las narrativas del terrario despliegan todo tipo de mundos donde la imaginación no tiene límites.

ANGLES+EARTH

www.anglesandearth.co.za ae_terrariums

Just like aquariums house water and aquatic plants, terrariums house earth and land flora. They are fascinating, educational, and contribute to the understanding of the principles of sustainable living. Denny Mo, the founder of Angles+Earth, is clear about his activity: He doesn't pot plants; he houses them in glass geometric forms. There is hardly any limit to what plant species can live inside a terrarium. To date, Angles+Earth has conquered desert, woodland and tropical terrains. The key to building a long-lasting terrarium is to understand the terrain and plant-life one is growing.

Tout comme les aquariums abritent l'eau et les plantes aquatiques, les terrariums abritent la terre et la flore terrestre. Ils sont fascinants, éducatifs et contribuent à la compréhension des principes d'un mode de vie durable. Denny Mo, le fondateur d'Angles+Earth, est limpide sur son activité : Il ne plante pas des plantes en pot, il les abrite sous des formes géométriques en verre. Il n'y a pratiquement pas de limite à ce que les espèces végétales peuvent vivre à l'intérieur d'un terrarium. À ce jour, Angles+Earth a conquis des terrains désertiques, boisés et tropicaux. La clé de la construction d'un terrarium de longue durée est de comprendre le terrain et la vie des plantes que l'on cultive.

So wie Aquarien Wasser und Wasserpflanzen beherbergen, beherbergen Terrarien Erde und Landflora. Sie sind faszinierend, lehrreich und tragen zum Verständnis der Prinzipien des nachhaltigen Lebens bei. Denny Mo, der Gründer von Angles+Earth, ist sich seiner Tätigkeit bewusst: Er tränkt keine Pflanzen, er beherbergt sie in geometrischen Glasformen. Es gibt kaum eine Grenze, welche Pflanzenarten in einem Terrarium leben können. Bis heute hat Angles+Earth Wüste, Wald und tropisches Terrain erobert. Der Schlüssel zum Bau eines langlebigen Terrariums liegt darin, das Gelände und die Pflanzenwelt zu verstehen, in der sie wächst.

Al igual que los acuarios albergan agua y plantas acuáticas, los terrarios albergan tierra y flora terrestre. Son fascinantes, educativos y contribuyen a la comprensión de los principios de la vida sostenible. Denny Mo, el fundador de Angles+Earth, es claro sobre su actividad: no planta en maceta, sino que las aloja en formas geométricas de vidrio. Apenas existe un límite para las especies de plantas que pueden vivir dentro de un terrario. Hasta la fecha, Angles+Earth ha conquistado el desierto, los bosques y los terrenos tropicales. La clave para construir un terrario duradero es entender el terreno y la vida vegetal que se esta cultivando.

PHOTOS © Angles+Earth

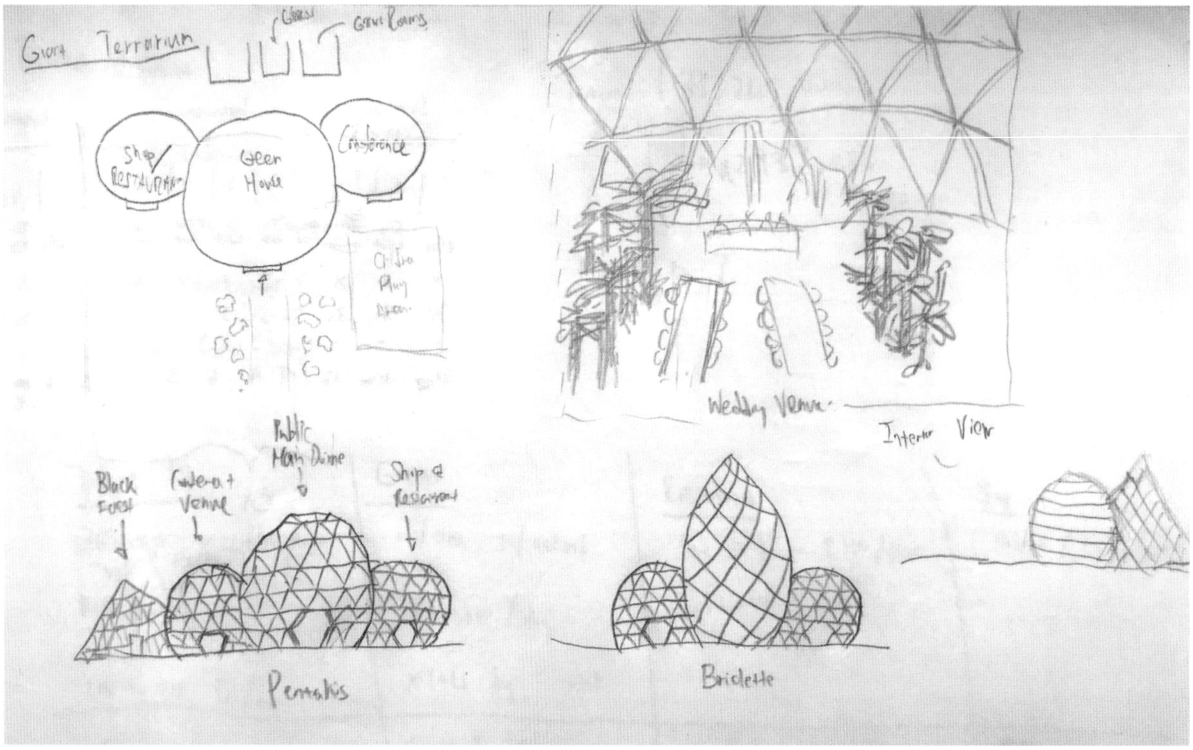

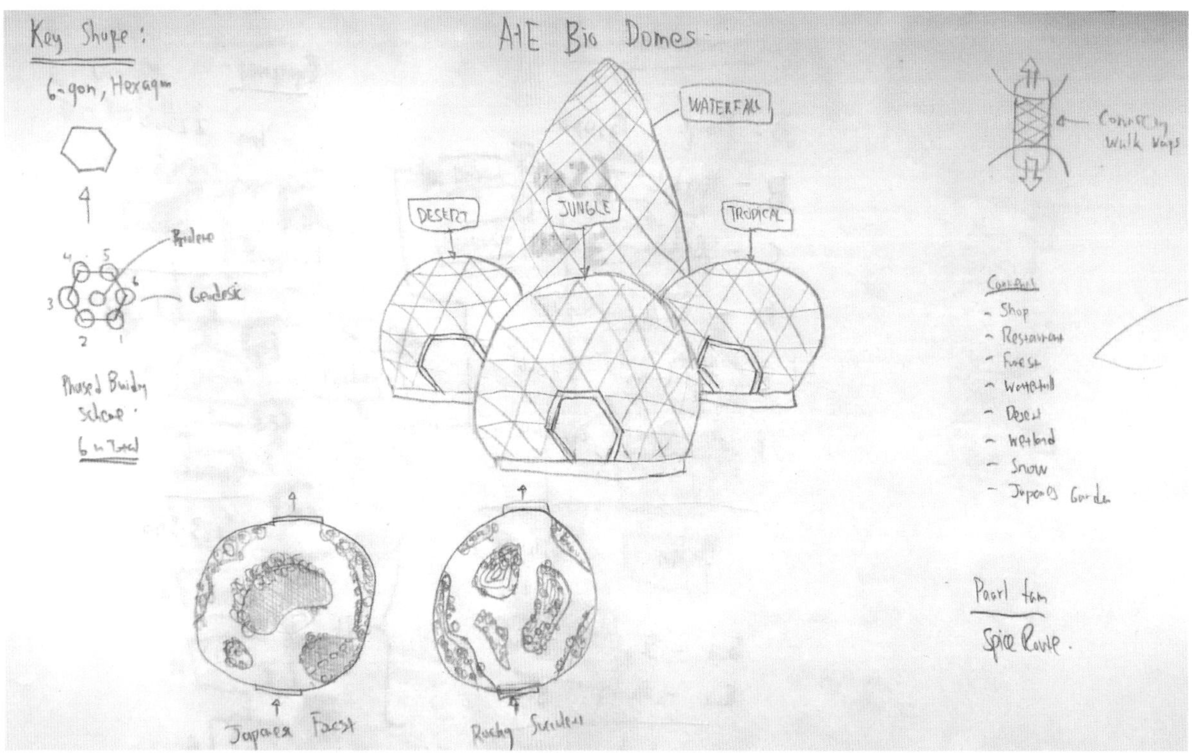

Africa's first bio-dome planning

Angles+Earth's automated terrariums are no longer dependent on their placement in relation to a sunny window thanks to a line of geometric stained glass designs incorporating a lamp. Briolette is both a terrarium and a lamp.

Die automatisierten Terrarien von Angles+ Earth sind dank einer Reihe geometrischer Glasmalereien mit einer Lampe nicht mehr von ihrer Platzierung in Bezug auf ein Sonnenfenster abhängig. Briolette ist sowohl ein Terrarium als auch eine Lampe.

Les terrariums automatisés d'Angles+Earth ne sont plus dépendants d'un emplacement près d'une fenêtre ensoleillée grâce à une ligne de vitraux géométriques avec une lampe intégrée. Briolette est à la fois un terrarium et une lampe.

Los terrarios automatizados de Angles+ Earth ya no dependen necesariamente de su ubicación en relación a una ventana soleada; una línea de vitrales geométricos incorporan una lámpara que proporciona la luz necesaria. Briolette es a la vez terrario y lámpara.

Automated terrariums incorporate an LED grow light coupled with a fan so that the terrarium doesn't overheat. Watering is still required, but the whole system can be controlled using a smartphone application to schedule the watering and switch the light on and off.

Automatisierte Terrarien verfügen über ein LED-Zuchtlicht, das mit einem Ventilator gekoppelt ist, damit das Terrarium nicht überhitzt. Die Bewässerung ist noch erforderlich, aber das gesamte System kann über eine Smartphone-Anwendung gesteuert werden, um die Bewässerung zu planen und das Licht ein- und auszuschalten.

Les terrariums automatisés intègrent une lumière de croissance LED couplée à un ventilateur pour que le terrarium ne surchauffe pas. L'arrosage est toujours nécessaire mais l'ensemble du système peut être contrôlé à l'aide d'une application smartphone qui permet de programmer l'arrosage, d'allumer et d'éteindre la lumière.

Los terrarios automatizados incorporan una luz de crecimiento LED junto con un ventilador para evitar sobrecalentamiento. El riego sigue siendo necesario, pero todo el sistema se puede controlar mediante una aplicación para programar el riego y encender y apagar la luz.

Love having fresh herbs at your fingertips, but don't have the space for a herb garden or time to tend it? Inspired by the Victorian glass cases, Angles+Earth has designed a modular herb garden that adapts to the users' needs and to the space available.

Sie lieben es, frische Kräuter zur Hand zu haben, haben aber nicht den Platz für einen Kräutergarten oder Zeit, sie zu pflegen? Inspiriert von den viktorianischen Glasvitrinen hat Angles+Earth einen modularen Kräutergarten entworfen, der sich an die Bedürfnisse der Nutzer und den verfügbaren Platz anpasst.

Vous aimez avoir des herbes fraîches à portée de main, mais vous n'avez pas l'espace pour avoir un jardin d'herbes ou le temps de vous en occuper ? S'inspirant des vitrines victoriennes, Angles+Earth a conçu un jardin d'herbes aromatiques modulaire qui s'adapte aux besoins des utilisateurs et à l'espace disponible.

¿Le encanta tener hierbas frescas al alcance de la mano, pero no tiene el espacio para un jardín interior o tiempo para cuidarlo? Inspirado en las vitrinas victorianas, Angles+Earth ha diseñado un jardín de hierbas modular que se adapta a las necesidades de los usuarios y al espacio disponible.

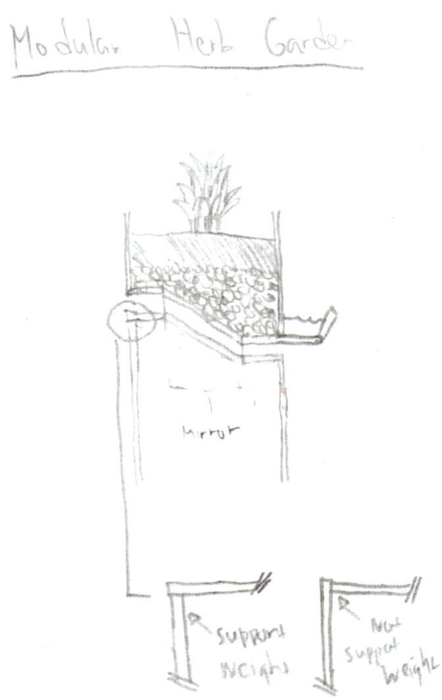

Modular herb garden

Angles+Earth is pushing the boundaries of stained glass. Their versatile "wallscapes" are designed to bring colour and life as well as to add dimension to walls while breaking away from the ordinary framed picture.

Angles+Earth erweitert die Grenzen der Glasmalerei. Ihre vielseitigen „Wallscapes" sind so konzipiert, dass sie Farbe und Leben in die Wände bringen, den Wänden eine Dimension verleihen und sich vom gewöhnlichen Rahmenbild lösen.

Angles+Earth repousse les limites du vitrail. Leurs «wallscapes» polyvalents sont conçus pour apporter de la couleur et de la vie, ainsi que pour donner de la dimension aux murs tout en s'éloignant de l'image encadrée ordinaire.

Angles+Earth trabaja al límite de la imaginación con los vidrios de colores. Sus versátiles "paisajes murales" están diseñados para dar color y vida, así como para añadir dimensión a las paredes, al tiempo que se alejan de la imagen enmarcada tradicional.

Sotto Bosco
Terrarium

SOTTOBOSCO TERRARIUM

www.sottoboscoterrarium.it   sottobosco_terrarium

Sottobosco started with Carlotta Tilli's desire to connect with nature, creating a microcosm where plants thrive the way they do in their natural habitat. Layers of soil, sand, pebbles, moss, and plants replicate the layers of the natural landscape on a macro scale, creating a similar environment for a micro landscape. These micro landscapes add a whole new dimension to indoor gardening while establishing a personal relationship with the natural world.

Sottobosco a commencé avec le désir de Carlotta Tilli de se connecter avec la nature, créant un microcosme où les plantes prospèrent comme elles le font dans leur habitat naturel. Des couches de sol, de sable, de cailloux, de mousses et de plantes reproduisent les couches du paysage naturel à une échelle macroscopique, créant un environnement similaire pour un micropaysage. Ces micro-paysages ajoutent une toute nouvelle dimension au jardinage intérieur tout en établissant une relation personnelle avec le monde naturel.

Sottobosco begann mit Carlotta Tillis Wunsch, sich mit der Natur zu verbinden und einen Mikrokosmos zu schaffen, in dem Pflanzen so gedeihen, wie sie es in ihrem natürlichen Lebensraum tun. Schichten aus Erde, Sand, Kieselsteinen, Moos und Pflanzen replizieren die Schichten der Naturlandschaft auf Makroebene und schaffen eine ähnliche Umgebung für eine Mikrolandschaft. Diese Mikrolandschaften verleihen dem Indoor-Gartenbau eine ganz neue Dimension und schaffen gleichzeitig eine persönliche Beziehung zur Natur.

Sottobosco comenzó con el deseo de Carlotta Tilli de conectarse con la naturaleza, creando un microcosmos donde las plantas prosperan como lo hacen en su hábitat natural. Las capas de tierra, arena, guijarros, musgo y plantas replican las capas del paisaje natural a una escala macro, creando un entorno similar para un micropaisaje. Estos micropaisajes añaden una nueva dimensión a la jardinería de interior, a la vez que establecen una relación personal con el mundo natural.

PHOTOS © Chiara Bocchino

Terrariums are not mere decorative pieces. They can be considered a creative journey or process of creation and care and observation. This process reveals the changes in growth and decay, reminding us of the vulnerability of nature and how important it is to care for it.

Les terrariums ne sont pas de simples pièces décoratives. Ils peuvent être considérés comme un voyage créatif ou un processus de création, de soin et d'observation. Ce processus révèle les changements dans la croissance et la décomposition, nous rappelant la vulnérabilité de la nature et l'importance d'en prendre soin.

Terrarien sind keine bloßen Schmuckstücke. Sie können als eine kreative Reise oder als Prozess der Schöpfung, Pflege und Beobachtung betrachtet werden. Dieser Prozess zeigt die Veränderungen in Wachstum und Verfall auf und erinnert uns an die Verletzlichkeit der Natur und wie wichtig es ist, sie zu pflegen.

Los terrarios no son meras piezas decorativas. Pueden ser considerados como un viaje creativo o un proceso de creación, cuidado y observación. Este proceso revela los cambios en el crecimiento y la decadencia, recordándonos la vulnerabilidad de la naturaleza y lo importante de su cuidado.

The Green label

www.facebook.com/thegreenlabelmy thegreenlabelmy

Glass provides a minimal barrier between the ideal ecosystem of the terrarium and the real world. While terrariums feature the beauty and life of Nature, they are also a reminder of its vulnerability. Terrarium design is not just a fun activity; it promotes environment and sustainable practice initiatives so necessary nowadays when we are becoming increasingly dependant on industrialisation and technology and far too disconnected from our natural surroundings.

Le verre constitue une barrière minimale entre l'écosystème idéal du terrarium et le monde réel. Si les terrariums mettent en valeur la beauté et la vie de la nature, ils sont aussi un rappel de sa vulnérabilité. La conception de terrariums n'est pas seulement une activité amusante, elle promeut des initiatives environnementales et des pratiques durables tellement nécessaires de nos jours, alors que nous sommes de plus en plus dépendants de l'industrialisation et de la technologie et trop éloignés de notre environnement naturel.

Glas bildet eine minimale Barriere zwischen dem idealen Ökosystem des Terrariums und der realen Welt. Terrarien zeigen die Schönheit und das Leben der Natur, erinnern aber auch an ihre Verletzlichkeit. Terrariengestaltung ist nicht nur eine unterhaltsame Aktivität, sondern fördert auch Umwelt- und nachhaltige Praxisinitiativen, die heutzutage so notwendig sind, sind wir doch zunehmend von Industrialisierung und Technologie abhängig und damit viel zu weit von unserer natürlichen Umgebung entfernt.

El vidrio proporciona una barrera mínima entre el ecosistema ideal del terrario y el mundo real. Además de mostrar la belleza y la vida de la naturaleza, los terrarios también son un recordatorio de su vulnerabilidad. El diseño de terrarios no es solo una actividad divertida, sino que promueve iniciativas medioambientales y prácticas sostenibles tan necesarias, en un momento en el que dependemos cada vez más de la industrialización y la tecnología y estamos demasiado desconectados de nuestro entorno natural.

PHOTOS © Aaron Fredericks

Perhaps, the desire to encapsulate a piece of Nature is a subconscious effort to care for and to protect her from humans' impetuous interaction with their surrounding environment.

Vielleicht ist der Wunsch, ein Stück Natur zu verkapseln, ein unbewusstes Bemühen, sie zu pflegen und vor den ungestümen Eingriffen des Menschen in seine Umwelt zu schützen.

Peut-être que le désir d'encapsuler un morceau de nature est un effort subconscient pour prendre soin d'elle et la protéger de l'interaction impétueuse des humains avec leur environnement.

El deseo de encapsular un pedazo de naturaleza puede ser un esfuerzo subconsciente para cuidarla y protegerla de la interacción impetuosa de los humanos.

If terrariums have enjoyed popularity for so long and are so attractive to people is clearly because humans have a subconscious connection with the natural world and show a special attraction to activities and things that are directly connected to Nature.

Si les terrariums jouissent d'une telle popularité depuis si longtemps et sont si attrayants pour les gens, c'est indubitablement parce que les humains ont une connexion subconsciente avec le monde naturel et montrent une attirance particulière pour les activités et choses directement liées à la nature.

Wenn Terrarien so lange Zeit beliebt waren und für den Menschen so attraktiv sind, liegt das daran, dass der Mensch eine unbewusste Verbindung zur Natur und eine besondere Anziehungskraft auf Aktivitäten und Dinge hat, die direkt mit der Natur verbunden ist.

Si los terrarios han gozado de popularidad durante tanto tiempo y son tan atractivos es claramente porque los humanos tienen una conexión subconsciente con el mundo natural y muestran una atracción especial por las actividades y cosas que están directamente relacionadas con la naturaleza.

Moss & Pebble

www.etsy.com/shop/mossandpebble   mossandpebble

Terrariums combine natural materials such as moss, stone, and wood to recreate the all-inspiring landscapes that we are all surrounded by. For apartment dwellers, terrariums are the closest to a garden of their own. Terrariums go beyond the mere assembly of plants, pebbles, seashells, and other decorative objects. They offer the opportunity for anyone to create their own ideal world, representing special moments and meaningful places.

Les terrariums combinent des matériaux naturels comme la mousse, la pierre et le bois pour recréer les paysages inspirants qui nous entourent tous. Pour les habitants d'appartements, les terrariums sont ce qui se rapproche le plus d'un jardin à eux. Les terrariums vont au-delà du simple assemblage de plantes, de cailloux, de coquillages et d'autres objets décoratifs. Ils offrent à chacun la possibilité de créer son propre monde idéal, représentant des moments privilégiés et des lieux significatifs.

Terrarien kombinieren natürliche Materialien wie Moos, Stein und Holz, um inspirierende Landschaften nachzubilden, von denen wir alle umgeben sind. Für Appartementbewohner kommen Terrarien einem eigenen Garten am nächsten. Terrarien gehen über die bloße Montage von Pflanzen, Kieselsteinen, Muscheln und anderen dekorativen Gegenständen hinaus. Sie bieten jedem die Möglichkeit, seine eigene ideale Welt zu erschaffen, die besondere Momente und bedeutungsvolle Orte repräsentiert.

Los terrarios combinan materiales naturales como el musgo, la piedra y la madera para recrear paisajes naturales de nuestro entorno. Para los habitantes de los apartamentos, los terrarios son lo más cercanos a un jardín propio. Los terrarios van más allá del mero ensamblaje de plantas, guijarros, conchas marinas y otros objetos decorativos. Ofrecen la oportunidad para que cualquier persona pueda crear su propio mundo vegetal ideal, representando momentos especiales y lugares significativos.

PHOTOS © Maria Solano

fish.
Matthew 4:19
UNDERWOOD

Large terrariums make excellent focal points. They do fulfil a decorative purpose, but they are also surrounded by an aura of unique peculiarity and captivation that invites to close examination.

Große Terrarien bilden hervorragende Schwerpunkte. Sie erfüllen einen dekorativen Zweck, sind aber auch von einer Aura einzigartiger Eigenart und Faszination umgeben, die zur genauen Betrachtung einlädt.

Les grands terrariums sont d'excellents points focaux. Ils remplissent une fonction décorative, mais ils sont aussi entourés d'une aura de particularité et d'enchantement unique qui invite à un examen attentif.

Los terrarios de gran formato son excelentes puntos focales. Cumplen una función decorativa, pero también están rodeados de un aura de peculiaridad y encanto únicos que invitan a una observación minuciosa.

When miniature figures are customised to represent familiar scenery, terrariums become much more than just a decorative item. They become a whimsical representation of moments to be remembered and, above all, they become priceless treasures.

Wenn Miniaturfiguren auf vertraute Landschaften zugeschnitten werden, sind Terrarien viel mehr als nur ein dekoratives Element. Sie werden zu einer skurrilen Darstellung von Momenten, die man sich merken muss, und vor allem zu unschätzbaren Schätzen.

Lorsque les figurines miniatures sont personnalisées pour représenter des paysages familiers, les terrariums deviennent bien plus qu'un simple objet décoratif. Ils deviennent une représentation fantaisiste de moments inoubliables et, surtout, ils deviennent des trésors inestimables.

Cuando las figuras en miniatura se personalizan para representar paisajes familiares, los terrarios se convierten en mucho más que un simple objeto decorativo, pasando a ser una representación caprichosa de momentos para recordar, de inestimables tesoros.

Ohsum mossum Terrariums

www.ohsummossum.com ohsummossum

Terrarium artists at Ohsum Mossum Terrariums regard plants as a gift of Nature while understanding their environmental requirements as well as their vulnerabilities. Ohssum Mossum offers terrarium workshops. They celebrate the green world, highlighting simplicity and naturalism while bringing people closer to Nature and raising people's environmental awareness. Terrariums, after all, are small samples of the bigger world we live in.

Les artistes des terrariums d'Ohsum Mossum Terrariums considèrent les plantes comme un don de la nature tout en comprenant les exigences environnementales ainsi que leur vulnérabilité. Ohssum Mossum offre des ateliers sur les terrariums. Ils célèbrent le monde vert, en mettant l'accent sur la simplicité et le naturalisme et en rapprochant les gens de la nature et en sensibilisant les gens à l'environnement. Après tout, les terrariums sont de petits échantillons du grand monde dans lequel nous vivons.

Terrarienkünstler in den Ohsum Mossum Terrarien betrachten Pflanzen als Geschenk der Natur und verstehen dabei sowohl ihre Umweltanforderungen als auch ihre Schwachstellen. Ohssum Mossum bietet Terrarien-Workshops an. Sie feiern die grüne Welt, betonen Einfachheit und Natürlichkeit, bringen die Menschen der Natur näher und schärfen das Umweltbewusstsein der Menschen. Terrarien sind schließlich kleine Kostproben der größeren Welt in der wir leben.

Los artistas de terrarios de Ohsum Mossum Terrariums consideran las plantas como un regalo de la naturaleza a la vez que comprenden sus requisitos medioambientales y sus vulnerabilidades. Ohssum Mossum ofrece talleres de terrarios. Celebran el mundo verde, destacando la simplicidad y el naturalismo, acercando a la gente a la naturaleza y elevando su conciencia ambiental. Los terrarios, después de todo, son pequeñas muestras del mundo en el que vivimos.

APP-TIONARY
FRESH PRODUCE

Terrariums are microcosms of the world outside, displaying the essence of Nature's ecosystems. Successful terrariums are often those that reflect an attentive observation of Nature.

Terrarien sind ein Mikrokosmos der Außenwelt und zeigen die Essenz der Ökosysteme der Natur. Erfolgreiche Terrarien sind oft solche, die eine aufmerksame Beobachtung der Natur widerspiegeln.

Les terrariums sont un microcosme du monde extérieur, montrant l'essence des écosystèmes de la nature. Les terrariums réussis sont souvent ceux qui reflètent une observation attentive de la nature.

Los terrarios son un microcosmos del mundo exterior que nos muestran la esencia de los ecosistemas. Los terrarios exitosos son aquellos que reflejan una atenta observación de la naturaleza.

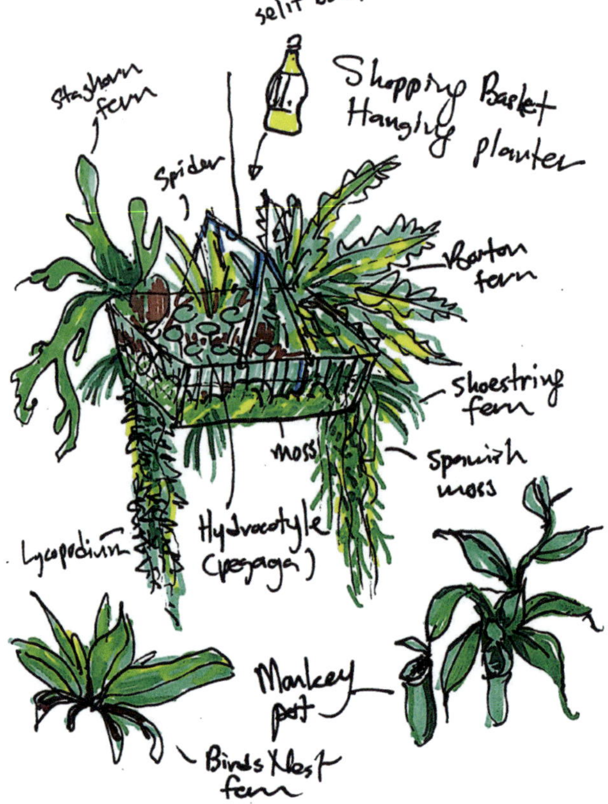

selit botol
Shopping Basket
Hanging planter
Staghorn fern
Spider
Boston fern
Shoestring fern
moss
Spanish moss
Lycopodium
Hydrocotyle (pegaga)
Monkey pot
Birds Nest fern

Terrariums are remarkable creations that reflect the sensibility of an artist. Like any other artistic process, making terrariums can involve drawing sketches to develop ideas and translate them into beautiful creations.

Terrarien sind bemerkenswerte Kreationen, die die Sensibilität eines Künstlers widerspiegeln. Wie jeder andere künstlerische Prozess kann die Herstellung von Terrarien das Zeichnen von Skizzen beinhalten, um Ideen zu entwickeln und diese in schöne Kreationen umzusetzen.

Les terrariums sont des créations remarquables qui reflètent la sensibilité d'un artiste. Comme tout autre processus artistique, la réalisation de terrariums peut impliquer de dessiner des croquis pour développer des idées et les traduire en de belles créations.

Los terrarios son creaciones notables que reflejan la sensibilidad de un artista. Como cualquier otro proceso artístico, hacer terrarios puede implicar dibujar bocetos para desarrollar ideas y traducirlas en bellas creaciones.

Soil composition, moisture level, and light are environmental factors that influence plant growth greatly. It is therefore key to sort and group plant specimens that respond to similar environmental conditions to ensure their survival and growth.

Bodenzusammensetzung, Feuchtigkeit und Licht sind Umweltfaktoren, die das Pflanzenwachstum stark beeinflussen. Daher ist es wichtig, Pflanzenproben, die auf ähnliche Umweltbedingungen reagieren, zu sortieren und zu gruppieren, um sowohl ihr Überleben als auch ihr Wachstum zu sichern.

La composition du sol, le taux d'humidité et la lumière sont des facteurs environnementaux qui influencent grandement la croissance des plantes. Il est donc essentiel de trier et de regrouper les spécimens de plantes qui répondent à des conditions environnementales similaires pour assurer leur survie et leur croissance.

La composición del suelo, el nivel de humedad y la luz son factores ambientales que influyen en gran medida en el crecimiento de las plantas. Por lo tanto, es fundamental clasificar y agrupar los especímenes vegetales que responden a condiciones ambientales similares para asegurar su supervivencia y crecimiento.

Exquisitely crafted scenery is enhanced by a sense of idealism and escapism elevating terrariums beyond mere plant arrangements contained in glass vessels into an art form.

Exquisit gestaltete Landschaften werden durch einen Sinn für Idealismus und Eskapismus bereichert, der Terrarien über bloße Pflanzenarrangements in Glasgefäßen hinaus zu einer Kunstform macht.

Les paysages d'une facture exquise sont rehaussés par un sens de l'idéalisme et de l'évasion qui élève les terrariums, au-delà de simples arrangements végétaux contenus dans des récipients en verre, au statut de forme d'art.

El paisaje exquisitamente trabajado es realzado por un sentido de idealismo y escapismo que eleva los terrarios a una forma de arte, más allá de las meras disposiciones vegetales contenidas en los recipientes de vidrio.

MOSSINGARDEN

www.mossingarden.com   mossingarden

Charles Loh is the founder of MOSSINGARDEN. His works are the result of his love and connection with nature. His childhood has fostered memories of fishing and camping trips. These memories awoke an interest in the natural world, an interest he managed to merge with a passion for art. With time he has mastered an artistic language through his fantastic creations to counterbalance the desensitisation caused by technology.

Charles Loh est le fondateur de MOSSINGARDEN. Ses œuvres sont le résultat de son amour et de son lien avec la nature. Son enfance lui a permis de se souvenir de voyages de pêche et de camping. Ces souvenirs ont éveillé un intérêt pour le monde naturel, un intérêt qu'il a réussi à fusionner avec une passion pour l'art. Avec le temps, il a maîtrisé un langage artistique à travers ses créations fantastiques pour contrebalancer la désensibilisation causée par la technologie.

Charles Loh ist der Gründer von MOSSINGARDEN. Seine Werke sind das Ergebnis seiner Liebe und Verbundenheit mit der Natur. Erinnerungen an intensive Naturerfahrungen wie Angeln und Campingreisen in der Kindheit haben sein Interesse an der Natur stets lebendig gehalten – ein Interesse, das er mit seiner Leidenschaft für die Kunst zu verbinden vermochte. Mit der Zeit hat er durch seine fantastischen Kreationen eine künstlerische Sprache entwickelt, deren Beherrschung der durch die Technisierung unseres Alltags verursachten Desensibilisierung entgegenwirken kann.

Charles Loh es el fundador de MOSSINGARDEN. Sus obras son el resultado de su amor y conexión con la naturaleza. Su infancia ha fomentado recuerdos de días pesca y salidas de acampada. Estos recuerdos despertaron un interés por el mundo natural, un interés que logró fusionar con una pasión por el arte. Con el tiempo ha dominado un lenguaje artístico a través de sus fantásticas creaciones para contrarrestar la insensibilización causada por la tecnología.

PHOTOS © Charles Loh

VOLUME

Nature is a wonderful world of forms, textures and colours. It encourages exploration, endlessly feeding creativity. As architect Frank Lloyd Wright said: 'Study nature, love nature, stay close to nature. It will never fail you.'

Die Natur ist eine wunderbare Welt aus Formen, Texturen und Farben. Sie fördert die Neugierde und nährt die Kreativität. Wie der Architekt Frank Lloyd Wright sagte: „Studiere die Natur, liebe die Natur, bleibe der Natur nahe. Sie wird dich nie enttäuschen."

La nature est un monde merveilleux de formes, de textures et de couleurs. Il encourage l'exploration, nourrissant sans cesse la créativité. Comme l'a dit l'architecte Frank Lloyd Wright : « Étudiez la nature, aimez la nature, restez proche de la nature. Elle ne vous décevra jamais. »

La naturaleza es un maravilloso mundo de formas, texturas y colores. Fomenta la exploración, alimentando sin cesar la creatividad. Como dijo el arquitecto Frank Lloyd Wright: "Estudia la naturaleza, ama la naturaleza, mantente cerca de la naturaleza. Nunca te fallará".

These wonderful pieces of nature encapsulated in glass vessels often tend to the rare, eclectic and mystical. They are objects that would not look out of place among other objects and artefacts such as antiques, art, shells and bones collections, and displays of desiccated insects.

Diese wunderbaren Naturstücke, die in Glasgefäßen verkapselt sind, neigen oft zum Seltenen, Eklektischen und Mystischen. Es handelt sich um Objekte, die neben anderen Objekten und Artefakten wie Antiquitäten, Kunst, Muscheln und Knochensammlungen oder Ausstellungen von ausgetrockneten Insekten nicht fehl am Platz sind.

Ces merveilleuses pièces de nature encapsulées dans des récipients en verre ont souvent tendance à être rares, éclectiques et mystiques. Il s'agit d'objets qui ne semblent pas déplacés parmi d'autres objets et artefacts comme des antiquités, des objets d'art, des collections de coquillages et d'os et des expositions d'insectes séchés.

Estas maravillosas piezas de la naturaleza encapsuladas en vasijas de cristal a menudo tienden a lo raro, ecléctico y místico. Son objetos que no parecerían fuera de lugar entre otros objetos e instrumentos como antigüedades, arte, colecciones de conchas marinas, de huesos o de insectos disecados.

ETERNIUM

www.etsy.com/au/shop/eterniumterrarium   eternium_terrarium

Terrariums are harmonious arrangements of plants. They are an ideal symbiosis of art and nature. Each terrarium is unique in the form and material of the container as well as in the selection of plants and their arrangement. Glass containers filled with lush greenery add a soft, soothing touch to a home. Undoubtedly, bringing some greenery, even contained, can satisfy the desire to be close to nature.

Les terrariums sont des arrangements harmonieux de plantes. Ils représentent une symbiose idéale entre l'art et la nature. Chaque terrarium est unique par la forme et le matériau du récipient ainsi que par le choix des plantes et leur disposition. Les contenants de verre remplis de verdure luxuriante ajoutent une touche douce et apaisante à une maison. Sans doute, apporter un peu de verdure, même contenue, peut satisfaire le désir d'être proche de la nature.

Terrarien sind harmonische Pflanzenarrangements. Sie sind eine ideale Symbiose aus Kunst und Natur. Jedes Terrarium ist einzigartig in Form und Material des Behälters sowie in der Auswahl der Pflanzen und deren Anordnung. Mit üppigem Grün gefüllte Glasbehälter verleihen einem Haus eine weiche, beruhigende Note. Zweifellos kann das Verlangen, der Natur nahe zu sein, dadurch befriedigt werden, dass man etwas Grün in seiner Wohnung findet.

Los terrarios son arreglos armoniosos de plantas; una simbiosis ideal de arte y naturaleza. Cada terrario es único en la forma y el material del contenedor, así como en la selección de las plantas y su disposición. Los recipientes de vidrio llenos de exuberante vegetación añaden un toque suave y relajante a la casa. Sin duda, traer algo de verdor, incluso en un recipiente, puede satisfacer el deseo de estar cerca de la naturaleza.

PHOTOS © Upstream Colour

ANTARCTIC
1982

Terrariums can be used in the same way one would use potted plants or a vase with cut flowers to dress up a room. They make for great decorative pieces, drawing attention through colour and texture.

Terrarien können auf die gleiche Weise genutzt werden, wie man Topfpflanzen oder eine Vase mit Schnittblumen verwendet, um einen Raum zu verschönern. Sie bilden großartige Dekorationsstücke, die durch Farbe und Textur auffallen.

Les terrariums peuvent être utilisés de la même manière que les plantes en pot ou un vase avec des fleurs coupées pour habiller une pièce. Ils donnent de superbes pièces décoratives et attirent l'attention par leurs couleurs et leurs textures.

Los terrarios se pueden utilizar de la misma manera que las plantas en maceta o un florero con flores cortadas para vestir una habitación. Son ideales para grandes piezas decorativas, ya que llaman la atención por su color y textura.

Terrariums are a decoration alternative to more usual plant displays such as those mentioned in the previous spread. Plants in terrariums, whether open or closed, definitely last more than cut flowers and just as long as potted plants, provided they are tended adequately.

Terrarien sind eine dekorative Alternative zu üblichen Pflanzenausstellungen, wie sie in der vorherigen Verbreitung erwähnt wurden. Pflanzen in Terrarien, ob offen oder geschlossen, halten definitiv länger als Schnittblumen und genauso lange wie Topfpflanzen, vorausgesetzt, sie werden ausreichend gepflegt.

Les terrariums sont une décoration alternative à l'utilisation de plantes plus habituelles telles que celles mentionnées dans la page précédente. Les plantes en terrarium, qu'elles soient ouvertes ou fermées, durent certainement plus longtemps que les fleurs coupées et aussi longtemps que les plantes en pot, à condition qu'elles soient bien entretenues.

Los terrarios son una alternativa decorativa a las exposiciones de plantas más habituales. Las plantas en terrarios, abiertos o cerrados, son más duraderas que las flores frescas y crecen tanto como las plantas en maceta, siempre y cuando estén bien cuidadas.

Meandry Natury

www.meandrynatury.pl   meandry_natury

Meandry Natury is a design studio that produces decorative items entirely made of natural materials, non-toxic, and handmade. Its goal is to introduce nature into peoples' daily lives while bringing a unique style into homes and public spaces. The unique plant arrangements created at Meandry Natury put an emphasis on the shape, following the principles of floral and decorative art.

Meandry Natury est un studio de design qui produit des objets décoratifs entièrement réalisés à partir de matériaux naturels et non toxiques et entièrement faits à la main. Son but est d'introduire la nature dans la vie quotidienne des gens tout en apportant un style unique dans les maisons et les espaces publics. Les arrangements végétaux uniques créés chez Meandry Natury mettent l'accent sur la forme suivant les principes de l'art floral et décoratif.

Meandry Natury ist ein Designstudio, das Dekorationsartikel herstellt, die vollständig aus natürlichen Materialien hergestellt, ungiftig und vollständig handgefertigt sind. Ziel ist es, die Natur in den Alltag der Menschen einzubringen und gleichzeitig einen unverwechselbaren Stil in Wohnungen und öffentlichen Räumen zu schaffen. Die einzigartigen Pflanzenarrangements von Meandry Natury betonen die Form und folgen den Prinzipien der Blumen- und Dekorationskunst.

Meandry Natury es un estudio de diseño que produce artículos decorativos totalmente hechos a mano de materiales naturales, no tóxicos. Su objetivo es introducir la naturaleza en la vida cotidiana de las personas y, al mismo tiempo, proponer un estilo único en los hogares y espacios públicos. Los singulares arreglos de plantas creados en Meandry Natury ponen énfasis en la forma, siguiendo los principios del arte floral y decorativo.

PHOTOS © Beata Kulig

Kokedama and Kusamono are two of Meandry Natury's field of interest. Both are very decorative forms of cultivation, bringing Nature indoors in its most artistic state. Kokedama and Kusamono are among the various gardening methods developed in Japan.

Kokedama und Kusamono sind zwei von Meandry Naturys Interessengebieten. Beide sind sehr dekorative Anbauformen, welche die Natur im Haus in ihren künstlerischsten Zustand bringen. Kokedama und Kusamono gehören zu den verschiedenen in Japan entwickelten Gartenmethoden.

Kokedama et Kusamono sont deux des domaines d'intérêt de Meandry Natury. Tous deux sont des formes de culture très décoratives, amenant la nature à l'intérieur des habitats dans son état le plus artistique. Kokedama et Kusamono font partie des différentes méthodes de jardinage développées au Japon.

Kokedama y Kusamono son dos de los campos de interés de Meandry Natury. Ambas son formas de cultivo muy decorativas, que llevan la naturaleza a los interiores en su estado más artístico. Kokedama y Kusamono son algunos de los diversos métodos de jardinería desarrollados en Japón.

Natural wall art or naturalistic panels are made of moss and other materials such as driftwood, branches, tree roots, bark, leaves, seeds, and pods. They are attractive and decorative objects inspired by Nature.

Natürliche Wandkunst oder naturalistische Paneele bestehen aus Moos und anderen Materialien wie Treibholz, Ästen, Baumwurzeln, Rinde, Blättern, Samen und Hülsen. Sie sind attraktive und dekorative Objekte, die von der Natur inspiriert sind.

L'art mural naturel ou les panneaux naturalistes sont faits de mousse et d'autres matériaux comme le bois flotté, les branches, les racines des arbres, l'écorce, les feuilles, les graines et les cosses. Ce sont des objets attrayants et décoratifs inspirés de la nature.

El arte mural natural o los paneles naturalistas están hechos de musgo y otros materiales como madera flotante, ramas, raíces de árboles, cortezas, hojas, semillas y vainas. Son objetos atractivos y decorativos inspirados en la naturaleza.

Terrariums are eye-catching but adding other elements such as coloured gravel can boost their visual appeal. These elements can be used to create contrast or to tie the terrariums with the rest of a room's décor.

Terrarien sind ein Blickfang, aber auch andere Elemente wie farbiger Kies können ihre Optik verbessern. Diese Elemente können verwendet werden, um Kontraste zu erzeugen oder um die Terrarien mit dem Rest der Raumdekoration zu verbinden.

Les terrariums attirent l'attention mais l'ajout d'autres éléments comme du gravier coloré peut renforcer leur attrait visuel. Ces éléments peuvent être utilisés pour créer un contraste ou pour lier les terrariums avec le reste du décor d'une pièce.

Los terrarios son de por sí llamativos, pero añadiendo otros elementos como la grava de colores aumentan su atractivo visual. Estos elementos se pueden utilizar para crear contraste o para ligar los terrarios con el resto de la decoración de una habitación.

Petite Jungle

www.petitejungle.de / www.facebook.com/petitejungleberlin   petitejungleberlin

Petite Jungle is a Berlin-based terrarium studio, founded by landscape architect Aurélie Morgen. What fascinates her the most? Terrariums are small self-sustaining ecosystems. From a scientific standpoint, the closed containers follow the principles of natural water cycles, involving processes of evaporation, transpiration, condensation, and precipitation. From a design viewpoint, Petite Jungle uses recycled glass or vessels found at flea markets and second-hand shops. The small gardens in glass can be found at her terrarium studio and at craft fairs and markets in Berlin.

Petite Jungle est un studio de terrarium basé à Berlin, fondé par la paysagiste Aurélie Morgen. Ce qui la fascine le plus ? Les terarium sont des petits écosystèmes autonomes. D'un point de vue scientifique, les contenants - et plus particulièrement les contenants fermés - suivent les principes des cycles naturels de l'eau impliquant les processus d'évaporation, de transpiration, de condensation et de précipitation. D'un point de vue design, Petite Jungle utilise du verre recyclé ou des récipients trouvés dans les marchés aux puces et les magasins de seconde main. Les jardins miniatures sous verre peuvent être achetés directement depuis l'atelier et dans les foires artisanales et les marchés de Berlin.

Petite Jungle ist ein Terrarienstudio mit Sitz in Berlin, das von der Landschaftsarchitektin Aurélie Morgen gegründet wurde. Was fasziniert sie am meisten ? Terrarien sind kleine, sich selbst erhaltende Ökosysteme. Aus wissenschaftlicher Sicht folgen die geschlossenen Systeme den Prinzipien des natürlichen Wasserkreislaufes mit den Prozessen der Verdunstung und Kondensation. Aus gestalterischer Sicht verwendet Petite Jungle Recyclingglas oder Gefäßen aus zweiter Hand, die auf Flohmärkten und in Gebrauchtwarenläden zu finden sind. Die Flaschengärten finden Sie im Terrarienstudio und auf Handwerksmessen und Märkten in Berlin.

Petite Jungle es un estudio de terrarios con sede en Berlín, fundado por la arquitecta paisajista Aurélie Morgen. ¿Qué es lo que más le fascina? Que los terrarios son pequeños ecosistemas autosuficientes. Desde el punto de vista científico, los contenedores cerrados siguen los principios de los ciclos naturales del agua, incluyendo procesos de evaporación, transpiración, condensación y precipitación. Desde el punto de vista del diseño, Petite Jungle utiliza vidrio reciclado o recipientes especiales que se encuentran en mercadillos y tiendas de segunda mano. Los pequeños jardines de cristal se pueden encontrar en el estudio de su terrario y en las ferias y mercados de artesanía de Berlín.

FIG. 662. DIEFFENBACHIA MAGNIFICA (see page 474).

FIG. 681. DRACÆNA GOLDIEANA.

Botanical illustrations from *The Illustrated Dictionary of Gardening,* authored by George Nicholson and published by L. Upcott Gill in London.

Herbaria and plant illustrations have scientific value but their aesthetic quality which cannot be ignored, has served as inspiration and continues to influence the works of many artists. It is only natural that terrarium artists would look at these collections of plants and drawings to find their inspiration.

Herbarien und Pflanzenillustrationen haben einen wissenschaftlichen Wert, aber ihre ästhetische Qualität, die nicht ignoriert werden darf, hat als Inspiration gedient und beeinflusst weiterhin die Werke vieler Künstler. Es ist nur natürlich, dass Terrarienkünstler sich diese Sammlungen von Pflanzen und Zeichnungen ansehen, um ihre Inspiration zu finden.

Les illustrations d'herbiers et de plantes ont une valeur scientifique, mais leur qualité esthétique, qui ne peut être ignorée, a servi d'inspiration et continue d'influencer les œuvres de nombreux artistes. Il est tout naturel que les concepteurs de terrarium puisent dans ces collections de plantes et de dessins pour trouver leur inspiration.

Las ilustraciones de herbarios y plantas tienen un valor científico, pero su calidad estética, que no puede ser ignorada, ha servido de inspiración y sigue influyendo en las obras de muchos artistas. Es natural que los artistas de terrarios miren estas colecciones de plantas y dibujos para encontrar su inspiración.

Miniature landscapes contained in glass jars are dramatic representations of the natural world. Not only has this art made its way into home decoration, but it has also awakened the creative inner self of some to reflect their personal relationship with nature.

Miniaturlandschaften in Gläsern sind dramatische Darstellungen der Natur. Diese Kunst hat nicht nur ihren Weg in die Wohnkultur gefunden, sondern auch das kreative innere Selbst einiger geweckt, um ihre persönliche Beziehung zur Natur zu reflektieren.

Les paysages miniatures contenus dans des bocaux de verre sont des représentations dramatiques du monde naturel. Non seulement cet art a fait son chemin dans la décoration intérieure, mais il a aussi éveillé la créativité intérieure de certains pour refléter leur relation personnelle avec la nature.

Los paisajes en miniatura contenidos en tarros de cristal son representaciones dramáticas del mundo natural. Este arte no solo ha llegado a la decoración del hogar, sino que también ha despertado el yo creativo interior de algunos para reflejar su relación personal con la naturaleza.

KOKEDAMADESIGN

kokedamadesign

Kokedama has made its way into home decor with an artistic take on houseplant display. In ancient Originally, Kokedama was a bonsai technique that involved taking the trees out of their pots exposing their roots. This technique celebrated the most natural and rough side of gardening. With time, this procedure evolved to become, perhaps, more manageable. The result is a natural container of moss and twine around the roots. Kokedama is just as beautiful as they are intricately elaborate creations, making unique focal points.

Kokedama s'est frayé un chemin dans la décoration de la maison avec une présentation artistique sur les plantes d'intérieur. Dans l'Antiquité, le Kokedama était une technique de bonsaï qui consistait à sortir les arbres de leurs pots en exposant leurs racines. Cette technique célébrait le côté le plus naturel et le plus brut du jardinage. Avec le temps, cette procédure a évolué pour devenir, peut-être, plus facile à gérer. Le résultat est un contenant naturel de mousse et de ficelle autour des racines. Kokedama produit des créations aussi belles que complexes et élaborées, et en font des points focaux uniques.

Kokedama hat seinen Weg in die Wohnkultur durch eine künstlerische Auseinandersetzung mit Zimmerpflanzen gefunden. Im Altertum war Kokedama ursprünglich eine Bonsai-Technik, bei der die Bäume aus ihren Töpfen genommen wurden, um ihre Wurzeln freizulegen. Diese Technik feierte die natürlichste und raueste Seite der Gartenarbeit. Sie entwickelte sich mit der Zeit zu einem eigenen, eher einfachen Verfahren. Das Ergebnis ist ein natürlicher Behälter mit Moos und Schnur um die Wurzeln herum. Kokedama ist genauso schön wie aufwendig ausgearbeitete Kreationen, die einzigartige Schwerpunkte setzen.

Kokedama se ha abierto camino en la decoración del hogar con una visión artística de la exhibición de plantas de interior. Originariamente, Kokedama era una técnica de bonsái que consistía en sacar los árboles de sus macetas exponiendo sus raíces. Esta técnica celebraba el lado más natural y áspero de la jardinería. Con el tiempo, este procedimiento evolucionó hasta convertirse, tal vez, en más manejable. El resultado es un contenedor natural de musgo y de cordel alrededor de las raíces. Kokedama es tan bello como lo son sus creaciones intrincadamente elaboradas, haciendo que sean puntos focales únicos.

PHOTOS © Aslı Aksoy Sezer

Kokedama can be enhanced by the form of display opening up a world of exciting gardening possibilities. These amazing botanical creations can be shown in a bowl or hanging from a string in mid-air for greater effect. Wabi-kusa is a variation on the theme of kokedama: water-loving plants are dipped into shallow water to grow naturally.

Kokedama kann durch seine Präsentation erweitert werden und eröffnet eine Welt voller aufregender Gartenmöglichkeiten. Diese erstaunlichen botanischen Kreationen können für mehr Wirkung in einer Schüssel oder an einer Schnur in der Luft gezeigt werden. Wabi-kusa ist eine Version von Kokedama: Wasser liebende Pflanzen werden in flaches Wasser getaucht, um natürlich zu wachsen.

Kokedama peut être amélioré par la forme de l'exposition qui ouvre un monde de possibilités de jardinage passionnantes. Ces étonnantes créations botaniques peuvent être présentées dans un bol ou suspendues à une ficelle en plein air pour plus d'effet. Wabi-kusa est une version du kokedama : les plantes qui aiment l'eau sont plongées dans des eaux peu profondes pour pousser naturellement.

Kokedama es una forma de exhibición que abre un mundo de posibilidades emocionantes de jardinería. Estas increíbles creaciones botánicas se pueden mostrar en un cuenco o colgando de una cuerda en el aire para obtener un mayor efecto. Wabi-kusa es una versión de kokedama: las plantas amantes del agua se sumergen en aguas poco profundas para crecer de forma natural.

HASS & CO BOTANICS

www.hassbotanics.com.au   hass_co_botanics

Hass Botanical offers a wide variety of plants and contemporary accessories that give the home the lush green feeling of nature. The wide botanical diversity ensures that there are plants for any indoor space, making them more inviting. Plants add to each other's beauty, creating artful compositions.

Hass Botanical offre une grande variété de plantes et d'accessoires contemporains qui donnent à la maison le sentiment vert et luxuriant de la nature. La grande diversité botanique fait qu'il y a des plantes pour tous les espaces intérieurs, ce qui les rend plus invitants. Les plantes s'ajoutent à la beauté de l'autre, créant des compositions artistiques.

Hass Botanical bietet eine große Auswahl an Pflanzen und zeitgenössischen Accessoires, die dem Haus das satte grüne Gefühl der Natur verleihen. Die große botanische Vielfalt sorgt dafür, dass es für jeden Raum einladende Pflanzen gibt. Pflanzen ergänzen sich gegenseitig in ihrer Schönheit und schaffen kunstvolle Kompositionen.

Hass Botanical ofrece una amplia variedad de plantas y accesorios modernos que dan a la casa la exuberante sensación de la naturaleza. La amplia diversidad botánica asegura que haya plantas para cualquier espacio interior, generando composiciones artísticas de gran belleza.

PHOTOS © Casey O'Callahan

In our increasingly developed urban environments, incorporating greenery in architecture give people the opportunity to reconnect with nature. Plants and trees bring a sense of unity between the buildings and the surrounding landscape.

In unserer zunehmend entwickelten städtischen Umwelt bietet die Einbeziehung von Grün in die Architektur den Menschen die Möglichkeit, sich wieder mit der Natur zu verbinden. Pflanzen und Bäume vermitteln ein Gefühl der Einheit zwischen den Gebäuden und der umgebenden Landschaft.

Dans nos environnements urbains de plus en plus développés, l'intégration de la verdure dans l'architecture donne aux gens l'occasion de renouer avec la nature. Les plantes et les arbres apportent un sentiment d'unité entre les bâtiments et le paysage environnant.

En los entornos urbanos cada vez más desarrollados, la incorporación del verde en la arquitectura nos ofrece la oportunidad de volver a conectarnos con la naturaleza. Las plantas y los árboles aportan una sensación de unidad entre los edificios y el paisaje circundante.

Houseplants infuse indoor spaces with life, bringing a breath of fresh air. They add colour and texture. Large plants work best in minimalist interiors where they don't overcrowd but make a powerful style statement. Small plants are versatile, combining well with other decorative items or displayed in groups for greater visual effect.

Zimmerpflanzen erfüllen Innenräume mit Leben und bringen einen Hauch von frischer Luft. Sie verleihen Farbe und Textur. Große Pflanzen eignen sich am besten für minimalistische Innenräume, in denen sie nicht überladend wirken, sondern ein kraftvolles Statement abgeben. Kleine Pflanzen sind vielseitig einsetzbar und lassen sich gut mit anderen Dekorationselementen kombinieren oder in Gruppen für eine bessere visuelle Wirkung präsentieren.

Les plantes d'intérieur insufflent de la vie dans les espaces intérieurs, apportant une bouffée d'air frais. Ils ajoutent de la couleur et de la texture. Les grandes plantes fonctionnent mieux dans des intérieurs minimalistes où elles ne sont pas surpeuplées mais où elles donnent un style puissant. Les petites plantes sont polyvalentes et elles se combinent bien avec d'autres objets décoratifs ou peuvent être disposées en groupes pour un meilleur effet visuel.

Las plantas de interior dan vida a los espacios interiores, aportando un soplo de aire fresco. Añaden color y textura. Las plantas grandes funcionan mejor en interiores minimalistas. Las plantas pequeñas son versátiles, pueden combinarse con otros elementos decorativos o estar expuestas en grupos para un mayor efecto visual.

Indoor spaces can contain greenery as a mean to bring nature into the home, whatever its size. Small spaces can hold planters that add style and enhance the plants they contain. No room for gardening? The Indoor Garden Tarp, designed by RT1Home (right), is ideal for re-potting plants in small spaces.

Les espaces intérieurs peuvent contenir de la verdure comme moyen de faire entrer la nature dans la maison, quelle que soit sa taille. Les petits espaces peuvent contenir des jardinières qui ajoutent du style et mettent en valeur les plantes. Pas de place pour le jardinage ? La Indoor Garden Tarp, conçue par RT1Home (à droite), est idéale pour rempoter les plantes dans les petits espaces.

Innenräume können Grün als Mittel enthalten, um die Natur in das Haus zu bringen, unabhängig von ihrer Größe. Kleine Räume können Pflanzgefäße aufnehmen, die Stil verleihen. Kein Platz für Gartenarbeit? Die von RT1Home (rechts) entworfene Indoor Garden Plane ist ideal für die Umtopfung von Pflanzen auf engstem Raum.

Los espacios interiores pueden contener vegetación como medio para llevar la naturaleza a la casa, sea cual sea su tamaño. Los espacios pequeños pueden contener jardineras que añaden estilo. ¿No hay espacio para la jardinería? RT1Home ha diseñado una lona de jardinería (derecha) ideal para trasplantar en espacios pequeños.

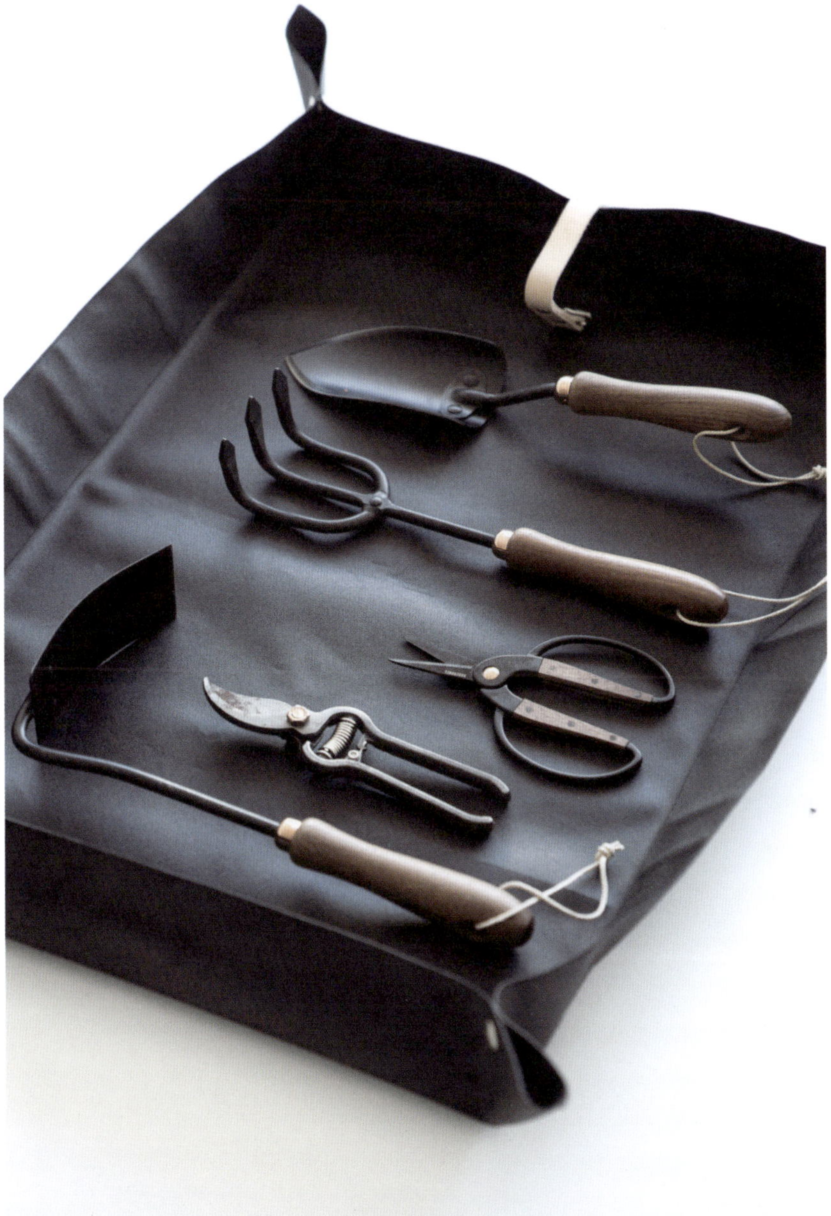

PLANT RUNNER
NEEM OIL

Hass & co
BOTANICS

© Richard Clarkson

Outside in Terrariums

www.facebook.com/outside.in.terrariums   outside.in.terrariums

Matthew Biffen founded Outside In Terrariums as a passion project in 2015 but soon became his Ikigai, which translates to "reason for being". This Japanese concept is based on four key principles: what you love, what you are good at, what the world needs, and what you can be paid for. Guided by these principles, Matthew combines his experience in graphic design with his love for nature to create unique works of living art. He works with a unique range of plants to create his terrariums, and hope to be a source of education for his customers and followers.

Matthew Biffen a fondé Outside In Terrariums comme projet passionnel en 2015, mais celui-ci est rapidement devenu son Ikigai, qui se traduit par «raison d'être». Ce concept japonais est basé sur quatre principes clés : ce que vous aimez, ce que vous savez faire, ce dont le monde a besoin et ce pour quoi vous pouvez être payé. Guidé par ces principes, Matthew combine son expérience en design graphique et son amour pour la nature pour créer des œuvres d'art vivantes uniques. Il travaille avec une gamme unique de plantes pour créer ses terrariums, et espère être une source d'enseignement pour ses clients et ses adeptes.

Matthew Biffen gründete Outside In Terrarien als Passionsprojekt im Jahr 2015, wurde aber bald zu seinem Ikigai, was übersetzt „Grund zum Sein" bedeutet. Dieses japanische Konzept basiert auf vier Schlüsselprinzipien: Was du liebst, worin du gut bist, was die Welt braucht und wofür du bezahlt werden kannst. Geleitet von diesen Prinzipien, kombiniert Matthew seine Erfahrung im Grafikdesign mit seiner Liebe zur Natur, um einzigartige Werke der Lebenskunst zu schaffen. Er arbeitet mit einer einzigartigen Auswahl an Pflanzen, um seine Terrarien zu gestalten, und hofft, eine Quelle der Bildung für seine Kunden und Anhänger zu sein.

Matthew Biffen fundó Outside In Terrariums como un proyecto apasionante en 2015, pero pronto se convirtió en su *Ikigai*, lo que se traduce en "razón de ser". Este concepto japonés se basa en cuatro principios: lo que amas, en lo que eres bueno, lo que el mundo necesita y lo que se te puede pagar. Guiado por estos principios, Matthew combina su experiencia en diseño gráfico con su amor por la naturaleza para crear obras de arte viviente únicas. Trabaja con una gama única de plantas para crear sus terrarios y espera ser una fuente de educación para sus clientes y seguidores.

GREENERY II
$675.00

Outside In Terrariums combines distinctive glassware and greenery to create high quality, handmade art pieces. They understand that apartment living is quickly becoming the norm, and with that, comes a demand for indoor plants that are low maintenance and sustainable.

Outside In Terrariums combine une verrerie distinctive et de la verdure pour créer des œuvres d'art de haute qualité, faites à la main. Ils comprennent que la vie en appartement devient rapidement la norme, et avec cela, vient une demande pour des plantes d'intérieur qui représentent un minimum d'entretien et qui sont durables.

Outside In Terrariums kombinieren unverwechselbares Glas und Grün zu hochwertigen, handgefertigten Kunstwerken und reagieren damit auf die steigende Nachfrage nach Zimmerpflanzen, die pflegeleicht und nachhaltig sind.

Outside In Terrariums combina la cristalería y el verde para crear piezas de arte de alta calidad hechas a mano. Entienden que la vida en apartamentos se está convirtiendo rápidamente en la norma, y como consecuencia, aumenta la demanda de plantas de interior de bajo mantenimiento y altamente sostenibles.

They are dedicated to protecting the world we live in, and sharing their message of conservation and respect for the environment. They believe in the importance of people's connection with Nature and hope to amplify this message through their designs.

Ils se consacrent à la protection du monde dans lequel nous vivons et partagent leur message de conservation et de respect de l'environnement. Ils croient en l'importance du lien des gens avec la nature et espèrent amplifier ce message à travers leurs créations.

Sie widmen sich dem Schutz der Welt, in der wir leben, und teilen ihre Botschaft des Schutzes und der Achtung der Umwelt. Sie glauben an die Bedeutung der Verbindung der Menschen mit der Natur und hoffen, diese Botschaft durch ihre Entwürfe zu verstärken.

Están dedicados a proteger el mundo en el que vivimos y a compartir su mensaje de conservación y respeto por el medio ambiente. Creen en la importancia de la conexión de la gente con la naturaleza y esperan amplificar este mensaje a través de sus diseños.

TERRARIUM DELIRIUM

terrarium.delirium

Terrarium Delirium was born from its creator's love for plants, nature, and the raw materials it provides. Terrarium Delirium brings a small representation of these materials into the urban environment, strengthening its connection with nature and promoting health and wellbeing. Working with natural materials offers moments of relaxation and enjoyment. There is also something marvellous about letting natural materials available at hand guide a design process toward the creation of fantastic tiny sceneries.

Terrarium Delirium est né de l'amour de sa créatrice pour les plantes, la nature et les matières premières qu'il fournit. Terrarium Delirium apporte une petite représentation de ces matériaux dans l'environnement urbain, renforçant son lien avec la nature et favorisant la santé et le bien-être. Travailler avec des matériaux naturels offre des moments de détente et de plaisir. Il y a aussi quelque chose de merveilleux à laisser les matériaux naturels disponibles à portée de main guider un processus de conception vers la création de fantastiques et minuscules paysages.

Terrarium Delirium wurde aus der Liebe seines Schöpfers zu Pflanzen, Natur und den von ihnen bereitgestellten Rohstoffen geboren. Terrarium Delirium bringt eine verkleinerte Darstellung dieser Materialien in die städtische Umgebung, stärkt die Verbindung zur Natur und fördert Gesundheit und Wohlbefinden. Die Arbeit mit natürlichen Materialien bietet Momente der Entspannung und des Genusses. Es ist auch etwas Wunderbares, wenn man natürliche Materialien zur Verfügung stellt, die einen Designprozess zur Schaffung fantastischer winziger Landschaften leiten.

Terrarium Delirium nació del amor de su creadora por las plantas, la naturaleza y las materias primas que proporciona. Terrarium Delirium aporta una pequeña representación de estos materiales en el entorno urbano, reforzando su conexión con la naturaleza y promoviendo la salud y el bienestar. Trabajar con materiales naturales ofrece momentos de relajación y disfrute. También hay algo maravilloso en dejar que los materiales naturales disponibles guíen un proceso de diseño hacia la creación de fantásticos paisajes diminutos.

PHOTOS © Mariana Mesquita

Even small glass containers filled with plants evoke the feeling of nature. They can go in any room of the home and are easy to care for. It is best, nonetheless, to start small working with simple plant arrangements and slowly expand the limits of one's creative possibilities using more plant varieties, moss and small rocks to add dimensionality.

Selbst kleine, mit Pflanzen gefüllte Glasbehälter wecken ein Gefühl von Natur. Sie können in jeden Raum des Hauses gehen und sind einfach zu pflegen. Es ist am besten mit einfachen Pflanzenarrangements zu arbeiten und langsam die Grenzen der eigenen kreativen Möglichkeiten zu erweitern, indem man mehr Pflanzensorten, Moose und kleine Steine verwendet, um die Dimensionalität zu erhöhen.

Même les petits récipients en verre remplis de plantes évoquent le sentiment de la nature. Ils peuvent aller dans n'importe quelle pièce de la maison et sont faciles à entretenir. Il est préférable de commencer avec des arrangements de plantes simples et de repousser lentement les limites des possibilités créatives en utilisant plus de variétés de plantes, de mousse et de petites roches pour ajouter de la dimensionnalité.

Incluso los pequeños recipientes de vidrio llenos de plantas evocan la sensación de la naturaleza. Pueden colocarse en cualquier habitación de la casa y son fáciles de cuidar. Lo mejor es empezar con arreglos de plantas sencillos y expandir lentamente los límites de las posibilidades creativas de cada uno utilizando más variedades de plantas, musgo y pequeñas rocas para añadir dimensionalidad.

Terrariums are tiny visions of larger worlds. It takes to be an artist to recreate the natural world outside, but mainly patience, foresight, and a vision of the final product.

Terrarien sind winzige Visionen größerer Welten. Es braucht einen Künstler, um die natürliche Welt draußen nachzubilden, aber vor allem Geduld, Weitsicht und eine Vision des Endprodukts.

Les terrariums sont de minuscules visions de mondes plus vastes. Il faut être un artiste pour recréer le monde naturel à l'extérieur, mais surtout de la patience, de la prévoyance et une vision du produit final.

Los terrarios son pequeñas visiones de mundos más grandes. Se necesita ser artista para recrear el mundo natural exterior, pero sobre todo paciencia, previsión y una visión anticipada de lo que resultará el producto final.

Teeny Tiny Terra

www.teenytinyterra.com   teenytinyterra

Teeny Tiny Terra's founder, Jesse Goldfarb, shares his passion for small plants through the creation of fantastic tiny gardens contained in the most unexpected vessels. This passion for small plants, which started with two bonsai, led Jesse to become a small plant collector and terrarium artist teaching tutorials throughout Toronto, Canada. According to Jesse, the terrarium trend will continue to expand as urban environments grow denser, and spaces become smaller.

Le fondateur de Teeny Tiny Terra, Jesse Goldfarb, partage sa passion pour les petites plantes à travers la création de jardins minuscules et fantastiques contenus dans les récipients les plus inattendus. Cette passion pour les petites plantes, qui a commencé avec deux bonsaïs, a amené Jesse à devenir un petit collectionneur de plantes et un artiste de terrarium proposant des tutoriels à Toronto, Canada. Selon Jesse, la mode des terrariums continuera de se développer à mesure que les milieux urbains se densifieront et que les espaces deviendront plus petits.

Der Gründer von Teeny Tiny Terra, Jesse Goldfarb, teilt seine Leidenschaft für kleine Pflanzen durch die Schaffung fantastischer winziger Gärten, die in den unerwartetsten Gefäßen enthalten sind. Diese Leidenschaft für kleine Pflanzen, die mit zwei Bonsais begann, führte Jesse dazu, ein kleiner Pflanzensammler und Terrarienkünstler zu werden, der in Toronto, Kanada, Tutorials underrichtet. Laut Jesse wird sich der Trend zum Terrarium weiter fortsetzen, wenn die städtische Umgebung dichter wird und die Räume kleiner werden.

El fundador de Teeny Tiny Terra, Jesse Goldfarb, comparte su pasión por las plantas pequeñas a través de la creación de fantásticos jardines diminutos contenidos en los recipientes más inesperados. Esta pasión por las plantas pequeñas, que comenzó con dos bonsáis, llevó a Jesse a convertirse en un pequeño coleccionista de plantas y artista de terrarios que enseña tutoriales en Toronto, Canadá. Según Jesse, la tendencia del terrario continuará expandiéndose a medida que los ambientes urbanos se vuelvan más densos y los espacios más pequeños.

Jesse often visits nurseries, thrift stores, and garage sales on the hunt for unusual glassware to house his tiny landscapes. Surprisingly, the most unexpected findings such as light bulbs, beakers, and test tubes lend to the creation of fantastic dioramas.

Jesse besucht oft Baumschulen, Gebrauchtwarenläden und Werkstattverkäufe auf der Suche nach ungewöhnlichem Glas für seine kleinen Landschaften. Überraschenderweise lassen sich mit den unerwartetsten Ergebnissen wie Glühbirnen, Bechern und Reagenzgläsern fantastische Dioramen erzeugen.

Jesse se rend souvent dans les pépinières, les friperies et les vide-greniers à la recherche d'objets en verre inhabituels pour abriter ses petits paysages. Étonnamment, les découvertes les plus inattendues comme les ampoules, les béchers et les éprouvettes permettent de créer de fantastiques dioramas.

Jesse a menudo visita viveros, tiendas de segunda mano y mercadillos en busca de cristalería inusual para albergar sus pequeños paisajes. Sorprendentemente, los hallazgos más inesperados, como bombillas, matraces y tubos de ensayo, contribuyen a la creación de fantásticos dioramas.

nice

The presence of plants in a home is often overlooked. They make a home feel lively. They also seem to have positive effects on people's mood and health. So why deny ourselves the enjoyment of plants when they come with such great benefits!

La présence de plantes dans une maison est souvent négligée. Elles font en sorte qu'une maison semble vivante. Elles semblent également avoir des effets positifs sur l'humeur et la santé des gens. Alors pourquoi nous priver du plaisir des plantes alors qu'elles offrent tant d'avantages !

Das Vorhandensein von Pflanzen in einem Haus wird oft übersehen. Sie sorgen dafür, dass sich ein Zuhause lebendig anfühlt. Sie scheinen auch positive Auswirkungen auf die Stimmung und Gesundheit der Menschen zu haben. Warum sollten wir uns also den Genuss von Pflanzen verkneifen, wenn sie mit so großen Vorteilen kommen!

La presencia de plantas en una casa a menudo se pasa por alto. Hacen que un hogar se sienta animado. También parecen tener efectos positivos en el estado de ánimo y la salud de las personas. Entonces, ¿por qué negarnos el disfrute de las plantas cuando generan tan grandes beneficios?

OZARIA TERRARIUMS & PLANTS

ozariaterrariumsandplants

Ozaria Terrariums & Plants started off as a side project that kicked off in 2018 with the concept of up-cycling unused glass containers and creating miniature live ecosystems within them, adding unique natural touches to indoor spaces. The idea is to personalise these indoor spaces, enticing people to design their own terrariums. The shop offers a wide range of terrariums with distinctive combinations of flora and personal totems as custom orders along with easy-to-care-for but exciting houseplants.

Ozaria Terrariums & Plants a commencé comme un projet parallèle qui a démarré en 2018 avec le concept de recyclage des récipients en verre inutilisés pour la création d'écosystèmes vivants miniatures, ajoutant des touches naturelles uniques aux espaces intérieurs. L'idée est de personnaliser ces espaces intérieurs tout en incitant les gens à concevoir leurs propres terrariums. La boutique propose une large gamme de terrariums avec des combinaisons originales de plantes et de totems personnels sur commande, ainsi que des plantes d'intérieur faciles d'entretien mais passionnantes.

Ozaria Terrarien & Pflanzen begann 2018 als Nebenprojekt mit dem Konzept des Upcyclings ungenutzter Glasbehälter und in ihnen miniaturisierte lebendige Ökosysteme zu schaffen, die den Inneräumen einzigartige natürliche Akzente verleihen. Die Idee ist es, diese Inneräume zu peronalisieren und die Menschen dazu zu verleiten, ihre eigenen Terrarien zu gestalten. Der Shop bietet eine große Auswahl an Terrarien mit einzigartigen Kombinationen aus Flora und persönlichen Totems auf Bestellung sowie pflegeleichte, aber spannende Zimmerpflanzen.

Ozaria Terrariums & Plants comenzó como un proyecto paralelo en 2018 con el concepto de reciclaje de envases de vidrio no utilizados y la creación de ecosistemas vivos dentro de ellos. La idea es personalizar estos espacios interiores, incitando a la gente a crear sus propios terrarios. La tienda ofrece una amplia gama de terrarios con combinaciones únicas de flora como pedidos personalizados junto con fascinantes plantas de interior de cuidado fácil.

Ozaria Terrariums & Plants own creations come in three different ranges: the AQUA range featuring a variety of aquatic plants and moss balls; the DESERT range, offering an assortment of succulents and cacti; and the FOREST range, providing a diversity of mosses and moisture-loving plants such as ferns.

Les créations d'Ozaria Terrariums & Plants se déclinent en trois gammes différentes : la gamme AQUA avec une grande variété de plantes aquatiques et de boules de mousse ; la gamme DESERT avec un assortiment de succulents et de cactus ; et la gamme FOREST avec une grande diversité de plantes qui aiment l'humidité comme les fougères.

Ozaria Terrarien & Pflanzen Eigenkreationen gibt es in drei verschiedenen Sortimentsbereichen: die AQUA-Serie mit einer Vielzahl von Wasserpflanzen und Mooskugeln, die DESERT-Serie mit einem reichen Sortiment an Sukkulenten und Kakteen und die FOREST-Serie mit mannigfaltigen Moosen und feuchtigkeitsliebenden Pflanzen wie Farnen.

Las creaciones propias de Ozaria Terrariums & Plants se presentan en tres gamas diferentes: la gama AQUA con una variedad de plantas acuáticas y bolas de musgo; la gama DESERT, que ofrece un surtido de suculentas y cactus; y la gama FOREST, que ofrece musgos y plantas amantes de la humedad, como los helechos.

The workshops give people full freedom of creativity, learning not only about upcycling and sustainability, but also learning about the relevant plant care. The results are unique pieces each time.

Les ateliers donnent aux participants toute liberté de créativité, leur permettant d'apprendre non seulement sur le cycle ascendant et la durabilité, mais aussi sur les soins à apporter aux plantes. Les résultats sont des pièces uniques à chaque fois.

Die Workshops geben den Menschen die volle Freiheit der Kreativität und vermitteln nicht nur Wissen über Upcycling und Nachhaltigkeit, sondern auch über die entsprechende Pflanzenpflege. Das Ergebnis sind jedes Mal Unikate.

Los talleres ofrecen plena libertad de creatividad, enseñando no solo acerca del reciclaje y la sostenibilidad, sino también sobre el cuidado de las plantas. Los resultados son piezas únicas.

FORET DE VERRE

www.foretdeverre.fr foretdeverre

Sébastien Boess founded Forêt de Verre in 2017. Initially passionate about permaculture and music, he embarked on this great adventure by chance, following a show on terrariums. Sébastien's creations are unique, and each is named after a musical piece. He uses a wide variety of recycled glass containers, transforming everyday trash into creative treasures. His continuous endeavour to find new ideas has recently led him to turn vintage collectables found in flea markets into homes for tropical plants.

Sébastien Boess a fondé Forêt de Verre en 2017. Passionné de permaculture et de musique, il s'est lancé dans cette grande aventure par hasard, après un spectacle en terrarium. Les créations de Sébastien sont uniques et chacune porte le nom d'une pièce musicale. Il utilise une grande variété de contenants de verre recyclé, transformant les déchets quotidiens en trésors créatifs. Ses efforts continus pour trouver de nouvelles idées l'ont récemment amené à transformer des objets de collection vintage trouvés dans des marchés aux puces en maisons pour plantes tropicales.

Sébastien Boess gründete 2017 Forêt de Verre. Zunächst leidenschaftlich für Permakultur und Musik entbrannt, geriet er durch Zufall nach einer Terrassenshow in dieses große Abenteuer. Die Kreationen von Sébastien sind einzigartig und jeweils nach einem Musikstück benannt. Er verwendet eine Vielzahl von recycelten Glasbehältern und verwandelt so den alltäglichen Müll in kreative Schätze. Sein ständiges Streben nach neuen Ideen hat ihn in jüngster Zeit dazu veranlasst, Vintage-Sammlerstücke von Flohmärkten in Häuser für tropische Pflanzen zu verwandeln.

Sébastien Boess fundó Forêt de Verre en 2017. Inicialmente apasionado por la permacultura y la música, se embarcó en esta gran aventura por casualidad, tras asistir a un espectáculo donde los terrarios eran protagonistas. Las creaciones de Sébastien son únicas, y cada una lleva el nombre de una pieza musical. Utiliza una gran variedad de contenedores de vidrio reciclado, transformando la basura diaria en tesoros creativos. Su continuo esfuerzo por encontrar nuevas ideas le ha llevado recientemente a convertir los coleccionables de época que se encuentran en los mercados de segunda mano, en hogares para plantas tropicales.

Each terrarium has a hand-carved wooden lid with a unique engraving. Sébastien focuses on readily available materials such as moss, wood, and stones that he collects in local forests but he also offers creations that fuse nature and technology. Plant jars with integrated solar collectors are one example.

Jedes Terrarium hat einen handgeschnitzten Holzdeckel mit einer einzigartigen Gravur. Sébastien konzentriert sich auf leicht zugängliche Materialien wie Moos, Holz und Steine, die er in den Wäldern der Region sammelt, aber er bietet auch Kreationen an, die Natur und Technik vereinen. Ein Beispiel sind Pflanzgefäße mit integrierten Solarkollektoren.

Chaque terrarium a un couvercle en bois sculpté à la main avec une gravure unique. Sébastien se concentre sur les matériaux facilement disponibles comme la mousse, le bois et les pierres qu'il collectionne dans les forêts locales, mais il propose aussi des créations qui allient nature et technologie. Les pots de plantes avec capteurs solaires intégrés en sont un exemple.

Cada terrario tiene una tapa de madera tallada a mano con un grabado único. Sébastien se centra en materiales fácilmente disponibles como el musgo, la madera y las piedras que recoge en los bosques locales, pero también ofrece creaciones que fusionan naturaleza y tecnología. Un ejemplo son los frascos de las plantas con colectores solares integrados.

© Oki Hiroyuki

POTE ATELIÊ BOTÂNICO

www.facebook.com/poteateliebotanico   pote_atelie_botanico

The founder of Pote Ateliê Botânico developed a strong connection with nature growing up on a farm. She remembers her mother cutting flowers from the garden to make flower arrangements. Attending architecture and urbanism school in São Paulo and later the floral art school Paulo Perissoto and Tanus Saab in Holambra, allowed her to look at the world of flowers in a way she hadn't done before. This new path allows her not only to create flower arrangements that suit her clients' needs and taste but also explore bold alternatives to traditional floral designs.

Le fondateur de Pote Ateliê Botânico a développé un lien fort avec la nature en grandissant dans une ferme. Elle se souvient que sa mère coupait des fleurs dans le jardin pour faire des arrangements floraux. L'école d'architecture et d'urbanisme de São Paulo et plus tard l'école d'art floral Paulo Perissoto et Tanus Saab à Holambra lui ont permis de voir le monde des fleurs comme elle ne l'avait jamais fait auparavant. Cette nouvelle voie lui permet non seulement de créer des arrangements floraux adaptés aux besoins et aux goûts de ses clients, mais aussi d'explorer des alternatives audacieuses aux motifs floraux traditionnels.

Die Gründerin von Pote Ateliê Botânico entwickelte eine starke Verbindung zur Natur. Sie wuchs auf einem Bauernhof auf und erinnert sich, dass ihre Mutter Blumen aus dem Garten geschnitten hat, um Blumenarrangements zu erstellen. Der Besuch der Architektur- und Städtebauschule in São Paulo und später der Blumenkunstschule Paulo Perissoto und Tanus Saab in Holambra ermöglichte es ihr, die Welt der Blumen auf eine Weise zu betrachten, wie sie es noch nie zuvor getan hatte. Dieser neue Weg ermöglicht es ihr, nicht nur Blumenarrangements zu kreieren, die den Bedürfnissen und dem Geschmack ihrer Kunden entsprechen, sondern auch mutige Alternativen zu traditionellen Blumenmotiven zu finden.

El fundador de Pote Ateliê Botânico desarrolló una fuerte conexión con la naturaleza al crecer en una granja. Recuerda a su madre cortando flores del jardín para hacer arreglos florales. Asistir a la escuela de arquitectura y urbanismo en São Paulo y más tarde a la escuela de arte floral Paulo Perissoto y Tanus Saab en Holambra, le permitió ver el mundo de las flores de una manera que no había visto antes. Este nuevo camino le permite no solo crear diseños florales que se adapten a las necesidades y gustos de sus clientes, sino también explorar alternativas audaces a los ejemplos más tradicionales.

PHOTOS © Karin Schnur Miotto

The shape of the containers guides the selection of plants. It is useful to know how big the plants will grow and how they will fill the container. The magic of terrariums doesn't last forever, though. Plants will eventually outgrow their small containers.

Die Form der Behälter bestimmt die Auswahl der Pflanzen. Es ist nützlich zu wissen, wie groß die Pflanzen werden und wie sie den Behälter füllen. Die Magie der Terrarien dauert jedoch nicht ewig. Pflanzen werden irgendwann aus ihren kleinen Behältern herauswachsen.

La forme des contenants guide le choix des plantes. Il est utile de savoir quelle taille les plantes vont pousser et comment elles vont remplir le contenant. La magie des terrariums ne dure pas éternellement. Les plantes finiront par dépasser leurs petits contenants.

La forma de los contenedores determina la selección de las plantas. Es útil saber qué tamaño tendrán las plantas y cómo llenarán el pequeño espacio. Sin embargo, la magia de los terrarios no dura para siempre; con el tiempo, las plantas superarán a sus pequeños contenedores.

Nature favours people's wellbeing. As we are spending more and more time indoors, tending plants at home brings us the much-needed connection with nature, while gives us satisfaction and stimulates creativity.

Die Natur fördert das Wohlbefinden der Menschen. Da wir immer mehr Zeit im Haus verbringen, bringt uns die Pflege der Pflanzen zu Hause die dringend benötigte Verbindung zur Natur, gibt uns Zufriedenheit und fördert die Kreativität.

La nature favorise le bien-être de l'homme. Comme nous passons de plus en plus de temps à l'intérieur, l'entretien des plantes à la maison nous apporte le lien tant attendu avec la nature, tout en nous donnant satisfaction et en stimulant la créativité.

La naturaleza favorece el bienestar. A medida que pasamos más tiempo en casa, el cuidado de las plantas nos conecta con la naturaleza, al mismo tiempo que nos da satisfacción y estimula la creatividad.

MADELEINE ORCHID

www.madeleineorchid.pl/obrazy-z-mchu/ madeleineorchid

Magdalena Zawadka's creations are not just the product of a hobby. She has a degree in horticulture and specialises in medicinal and tropical plants. This is one of those cases where a passion for plants turns into a professional career. Magdalena makes the most of the knowledge she has acquired, creating exquisite mini landscapes with a wide variety of plants. Her favourites, though, are orchids.

Magdalena Zawadkas Kreationen sind nicht nur das Ergebnis eines Hobbys. Sie ist diplomierte Gartenbauerin und spezialisiert auf Heil- und Tropenpflanzen. Dies ist einer der Fälle, in denen die Leidenschaft für Pflanzen in eine professionelle Karriere gemündet hat. Magdalena nutzt ihr erworbenes Wissen und schafft exquisite Miniaturlandschaften mit einer Vielzahl von Pflanzen. Ihre Favoriten sind jedoch Orchideen.

Les créations de Magdalena Zawadka ne sont pas seulement le fruit d'un hobby. Diplômée en horticulture, elle est spécialisée dans les plantes médicinales et tropicales. C'est un de ces cas où la passion pour les plantes se transforme en carrière professionnelle. Magdalena tire le meilleur parti des connaissances qu'elle a acquises en créant des mini-paysages exquis avec une grande variété de plantes. Ses préférées, cependant, sont les orchidées.

Las creaciones de Magdalena Zawadka no son solo el producto de un *hobby*. Es licenciada en horticultura y está especializada en plantas medicinales y tropicales. Este es uno de esos casos en los que la pasión por las plantas se convierte en una carrera profesional. Magdalena aprovecha los conocimientos adquiridos, creando exquisitos minipaisajes con una gran variedad de plantas. Sus favoritas, sin embargo, son las orquídeas.

The small scale of terrariums seems to offer the opportunity to create something that is real and unreal at the same time. Terrariums give those who make them —and those who own them to a lesser degree— a sense of control in the chaotic and fast-changing world we live in.

Der kleine Umfang der Terrarien bietet die Möglichkeit, etwas zu schaffen, das real und unwirklich zugleich scheint. Terrarien geben denen, die sie herstellen – und in geringerem Maße denen, die sie besitzen – ein Gefühl der Kontrolle in der chaotischen und sich schnell verändernden Welt, in der wir leben.

La petite échelle des terrariums semble offrir l'opportunité de créer quelque chose de réel et d'irréel à la fois. Les terrariums donnent à ceux qui en font – et à ceux qui les possèdent à un degré moindre – un sentiment de contrôle dans le monde chaotique et en rapide évolution dans lequel nous vivons.

La pequeña escala de los terrarios parece ofrecer la oportunidad de crear algo que es real e irreal al mismo tiempo. Los terrarios dan a los que los hacen –y en menor medida a los que los poseen– un sentido de control del mundo caótico y cambiante en el que vivimos.

The selection of a container is as important as that of plants. The two should not be regarded separately but as two items that complement each other to create a visually harmonious combination.

Le choix d'un contenant est aussi important que celui des plantes. Les deux ne doivent pas être considérés séparément mais comme deux éléments qui se complètent l'un l'autre pour créer une combinaison visuellement harmonieuse.

Die Auswahl eines Behälters ist ebenso wichtig wie die von Pflanzen. Beide sollten nicht getrennt betrachtet werden, sondern als zwei Elemente, die sich gegenseitig ergänzen, um eine optisch harmonische Kombination zu schaffen.

La selección de un contenedor es tan importante como la de las plantas. Los dos no deben considerarse por separado, sino como dos elementos que se complementan entre sí para crear una combinación visualmente armoniosa.

Closed terrariums create a warm and humid environment that is only suitable for moisture-loving plants. Once the plants are established, they require minimal care as they create their own self-sustaining ecosystem. Small ferns, ivy, and moss are among the numerous choices that thrive in humid conditions.

Geschlossene Terrarien schaffen eine warme und feuchte Umgebung, die nur für feuchtigkeitsliebende Pflanzen geeignet ist. Sobald die Pflanzen gesetzt sind, benötigen sie nur noch minimale Pflege, da sie ihr eigenes, selbsttragendes Ökosystem schaffen. Kleine Farne, Efeu und Moos gehören zu den zahlreichen Pflanzen, die unter feuchten Bedingungen gedeihen.

Les terrariums fermés créent un environnement chaud et humide qui ne convient qu'aux plantes qui aiment l'humidité. Une fois que les plantes sont établies, elles nécessitent un minimum de soins car elles créent leur propre écosystème autonome. Les petites fougères, le lierre et la mousse sont parmi les nombreux choix qui prospèrent dans des conditions humides.

Los terrarios cerrados crean un ambiente cálido y húmedo que solo es adecuado para plantas que aman la humedad. Una vez que las plantas están en fase de crecimiento, requerirán un cuidado mínimo ya que crean su propio ecosistema autosuficiente. Los helechos pequeños, la hiedra y el musgo son algunas de las numerosas opciones que prosperan en condiciones húmedas.

While they are mainly decorative, terrariums still maintain their original function as miniature greenhouses used to transport plants in safe conditions. Terrariums are portable, and as such, they can be moved from one place to another without much disruption.

Während sie hauptsächlich dekorativ sind, behalten Terrarien ihre ursprüngliche Funktion als Mini-Gewächshäuser, in denen Pflanzen unter sicheren Bedingungen transportiert werden. Terrarien sind tragbar und können daher ohne große Schwierigkeiten von einem Ort zum anderen verschoben werden.

Bien qu'ils soient principalement décoratifs, les terrariums conservent leur fonction originelle de serres miniatures utilisées pour transporter les plantes dans des conditions sûres. Les terrariums sont portatifs et peuvent donc être déplacés d'un endroit à l'autre sans trop de perturbations.

Si bien son principalmente decorativos, los terrarios siguen manteniendo su función original de invernaderos en miniatura utilizados para transportar plantas en condiciones seguras. Los terrarios son portátiles, y como tales, pueden ser trasladados de un lugar a otro sin ningún problema.

TERRACHIC

www.terrachic.co.uk terrachic_uk

Joanne Powles is a researcher and lecturer specialising in animal science. 'I am a behavioural ecologist', she says. Her job has more to do with animals than with plants, but as a child, she was fascinated by unusual plants and kept cacti and carnivorous plants on her bedroom windowsill. She has always loved the look of plants under glass, whether under a cloche, in a greenhouse or planted in a terrarium. After starting a family, her growing interest in terrarium making turned into a business venture, one, which luckily, fitted around her children's school and activities.

Joanne Powles combine sa carrière en sciences animales en tant que chercheuse et conférencière. « Je suis une écologiste comportementale », dit-elle. Son travail concerne plus les animaux que les plantes, mais elle a toujours aimé l'aspect des plantes sous verre, que ce soit sous cloche, dans une serre ou dans un terrarium. Enfant, elle était fascinée par les plantes inhabituelles et autant d'enfants gardaient des cactus et des plantes carnivores sur le rebord de la fenêtre de sa chambre. Après avoir fondé une famille, elle voulait trouver quelque chose qui s'intégrait bien à l'école et aux clubs d'enfants, et elle était très enthousiaste à l'idée de se lancer dans une entreprise commerciale.

Joanne Powles verfolgt eine tierwissenschaftliche Karriere als Forscherin und Dozentin. „Ich bin eine Verhaltensökologin", sagt sie über sich selbst. Ihre Arbeit hat zwar mehr mit Tieren als mit Pflanzen zu tun, aber sie hat immer das Aussehen von Pflanzen unter Glas geliebt, sei es unter einer Glocke, im Gewächshaus oder im Terrarium. Als Kind war sie von ungewöhnlichen Pflanzen fasziniert und so viele Kinder hielten Kakteen und fleischfressende Pflanzen auf ihrer Fensterbank im Schlafzimmer. Nachdem sie eine Familie gegründet hatte, wollte sie etwas finden, das in die Umgebung von Schule und Kinderclubs passte und war sehr daran interessiert, sich an einem Geschäftsvorhaben zu beteiligen.

Joanne Powles combina su carrera en ciencias animales trabajando como investigadora y profesora. "Soy una ecologista del comportamiento". Su trabajo tiene más que ver con los animales que con las plantas, pero siempre le ha gustado el aspecto de las plantas dentro de un contenedor de vidrio, ya sea bajo una campana, en un invernadero o plantadas en un terrario. Cuando era niña, le fascinaban las plantas inusuales y como muchos otros niños mantenían cactus y plantas carnívoras en el alféizar de la ventana de su habitación. Después de formar una familia, quería encontrar algo que encajara en la escuela y en los clubes infantiles y que a la vez le sirviera como modo de ganarse la vida.

PHOTOS © Joanne Powles

£12
Love

Joanne tries to make her terrariums look as natural as possible as if a little slice of land has been taken and transplanted, whether it be desert, woodland or tropical forest. She uses multiple colours and sizes of gravel to add depth and texture to her designs as well as features such as pebbles and driftwood to add interest.

Joanne versucht, ihre Terrarien so natürlich wie möglich aussehen zu lassen, als ob ein kleines Stück Land genommen und verpflanzt worden wäre, sei es Wüste, Wald oder Tropenwald. Sie verwendet mehrere Farben und Größen von Kies, um ihren Designs Tiefe und Textur zu verleihen, sowie Accessoires wie Kieselsteine und Holz, um Interesse zu wecken.

Joanne essaie de rendre ses terrariums aussi naturels que possible, comme si une petite parcelle de terre avait été prise et transplantée, que ce soit un désert, une forêt ou une forêt tropicale. Elle utilise de multiples couleurs et tailles de gravier pour ajouter de la profondeur et de la texture à ses dessins ainsi que des caractéristiques comme les cailloux et le bois pour ajouter de l'intérêt.

Joanne trata de hacer que sus terrarios se vean tan naturales como sea posible, como si una pequeña porción de tierra hubiera sido tomada y transplantada, ya sea parte de un desierto, de un bosque o de una selva tropical. Utiliza múltiples colores y tamaños de grava, guijarros y trozos de madera para añadir profundidad y textura a sus diseños.

Open or closed, terrariums respond to the environmental requirements of different plants. Enclosed terrariums create an ecosystem with a water cycle that is ideal for moisture-loving plants. Open terrariums don't have a water cycle. They are, therefore, suitable for plants that thrive in dry conditions but still require occasional watering.

Offene oder geschlossene Terrarien reagieren auf die Umweltanforderungen verschiedener Biotope. Geschlossene Terrarien schaffen ein Ökosystem mit einem Wasserkreislauf, der ideal für feuchtigkeitsliebende Pflanzen ist. Offene Terrarien haben keinen Wasserkreislauf; sie sind daher für Pflanzen geeignet, die unter trockenen Bedingungen gedeihen, aber dennoch gelegentlich bewässert werden müssen.

Les terrariums ouverts ou fermés répondent aux exigences environnementales des différentes plantes. Les terrariums fermés créent un écosystème avec cycle de l'eau idéal pour les plantes qui aiment l'humidité. Les terrariums ouverts n'ont pas de cycle de l'eau. Ils conviennent donc aux plantes qui poussent dans des conditions sèches mais qui nécessitent encore un arrosage occasionnel.

Los terrarios abiertos o cerrados responden a las exigencias medioambientales de las diferentes plantas. Los terrarios cerrados crean un ecosistema con un ciclo del agua que es ideal para las plantas amantes de la humedad. Los terrarios abiertos no tienen ciclo de agua y son por tanto adecuados para plantas que crecen en condiciones secas pero que requieren riego ocasional.

Air plants are extremely versatile. Joanne offers people the pleasure of designing their own air plant terrarium with practical air plant kits. They come with two different air plants —one of which is growing on driftwood— and all of the gravel, moss, and shells needed to create a beautiful display.

Luftpflanzen sind äußerst vielseitig einsetzbar. Joanne bietet den Menschen das Vergnügen, ihr eigenes Terrarium mit praktischen Luftpflanzenkits zu gestalten. Sie werden mit zwei verschiedenen Luftpflanzen geliefert – eine davon wächst auf Holz – und mit allen Kies, Moos und Muscheln, die für eine schöne Präsentation benötigt werden.

Les plantes à air sont extrêmement polyvalentes. Joanne offre aux gens le plaisir de concevoir leur propre terrarium avec des trousses pratiques pour plantes à air. Ils sont livrés avec deux plantes à air différentes – dont l'une pousse sur du bois – et tout le gravier, mousse et coquillages nécessaires pour créer une belle présentation.

Las "plantas de aire" son extremadamente versátiles. Joanne ofrece al cliente el placer de diseñar su propio terrario con unos prácticos kits que incluyen dos plantas diferentes –una de las cuales crece sobre madera– y toda la gravilla, el musgo y las conchas necesarias para crear una hermosa presentación.

MOSSWORKSHOP

https://m.facebook.com/mossworkshop   mossworkshop

Hiking and admiration for nature is the inspiration source for the designer at Mossworkshop. He is particularly interested in moss and always keeps an attentive eye to take in the beauty of these plants. This close observation has encouraged him to learn more about the world of mosses. For instance, although mosses are small and inconspicuous, they are a lot stronger than they look and they only grow in places with excellent air quality.

La randonnée et l'admiration pour la nature sont la source d'inspiration du designer de Mossworkshop. Il s'intéresse particulièrement à la mousse et garde toujours un œil attentif qui lui permet d'apprécier la beauté de ces plantes. Cette observation attentive l'a encouragé à en apprendre davantage sur le monde des mousses. Par exemple, bien que les mousses soient petites et discrètes, elles sont beaucoup plus résistantes qu'elles n'en ont l'air et ne poussent que dans des endroits où la qualité de l'air est excellente.

Wandern und Bewunderung für die Natur ist die Inspirationsquelle für den Designer des Mossworkshops. Er interessiert sich besonders für Moos und achtet immer darauf, die Schönheit dieser Pflanzen zu entdecken. Diese genaue Beobachtung hat ihn ermutigt, mehr über die Welt der Moose zu erfahren. Zum Beispiel: obwohl Moose klein und unauffällig sind, sind sie viel stärker, als sie aussehen, und sie wachsen nur an Orten mit hervorragender Luftqualität.

El senderismo y la admiración por la naturaleza son la fuente de inspiración del diseñador de Mossworkshop, particularmente interesado en el musgo y siempre atento para captar la belleza de estas plantas. Esta observación cercana le ha animado a aprender más sobre el mundo de los musgos. Aunque los musgos son pequeños y discretos, son mucho más fuertes de lo que parecen y solo crecen en lugares con excelente calidad de aire.

PHOTOS © Mossworkshop

Moss is the main element in the terrariums created at Mossworkshop. The goal is to educate others about this little known plant and foster awareness about the critical role of moss in the wellbeing of natural ecosystems.

La mousse est l'élément principal des terrariums créés par Mossworkshop. L'objectif est d'éduquer la population sur cette plante peu connue et de la sensibiliser au rôle crucial de la mousse pour le bien-être des écosystèmes naturels.

Moos ist das Hauptelement in den Terrarien der Mossworkshop. Ziel ist es, andere über diese wenig bekannte Pflanze aufzuklären und das Bewusstsein für die entscheidende Rolle des Mooses für das Wohlbefinden der natürlichen Ökosysteme zu fördern.

El musgo es el elemento principal de los terrarios creados en Mossworkshop. El objetivo es educar a otros sobre esta planta poco conocida y fomentar la conciencia sobre el papel crucial del musgo en el bienestar de los ecosistemas naturales.

BEST MOSS

BEST_MOSS

Mosses are bryophytes, which are the most primitive land plant. Ferns are also plants. They differ from mosses in that they are vascular plants and they are also different from other plants because they don't produce seeds or flowers. Best Moss embraces the world of these, perhaps, lesser-known plants, keeping a photographic record of his observations.

Les mousses sont des bryophytes, qui sont les plantes terrestres les plus primitives.
Les fougères sont aussi des plantes. Elles diffèrent des mousses en ce qu'elles sont des plantes vasculaires et elles sont également différentes des autres plantes parce qu'elles ne produisent pas de graines ou de fleurs. Best Moss embrasse le monde de ces plantes, peut-être moins connues, en gardant une trace photographique de ses observations.

Moose sind Bryophyten und gehören damit zu den primitivsten Landpflanzen.
Farne sind auch Pflanzen, jedoch, anders als Moose, sogenannte Gefäßpflanzen. Im Unterschied zu anderen Pflanzen produzieren Farne keine Samen oder Blüten. Best Moss umarmt die Welt dieser vielleicht weniger bekannten Pflanzen und hält seine Beobachtungen fotografisch fest.

Los musgos son briofitas, la planta terrestre más primitiva.
Los helechos también son plantas. Se diferencian de los musgos en que son plantas vasculares y también se diferencian de otras plantas porque no producen semillas ni flores. Best Moss abarca el mundo de estas plantas menos conocidas, manteniendo un registro fotográfico de sus observaciones.

PHOTOS © Hamid Hajian

Mosses have a mysterious aura. This could be attributed not just to the fact that they are the most primitive plants on land, but also because we generally find them in shaded and damp woods, covering decaying logs and clinging to rocks. Under our astonished eyes, they create mesmerizing maps of colonies.

Les mousses ont une aura mystérieuse. Cela pourrait être attribué non seulement au fait qu'il s'agit des plantes les plus primitives sur terre, mais aussi à l'endroit où l'on les trouve généralement, dans des bois ombragés et humides, couvrant les billes en décomposition et s'accrochant aux rochers. Sous nos yeux étonnés, elles créent des cartes fascinantes des colonies.

Moose haben eine mysteriöse Aura. Dies ist nicht nur darauf zurückzuführen, dass sie die primitivsten Pflanzen an Land sind, sondern auch darauf, dass wir sie in der Regel in schattigen und feuchten Wäldern finden, die verrottende Stämme bedecken und sich an Felsen festsetzen. Vor unseren staunenden Augen bilden ihre Kolonien faszinierende Landkarten.

Los musgos tienen un aura misteriosa. Esto puede atribuirse no solo al hecho de que son las plantas más primitivas de la tierra, sino también porque solemos encontrarlas en bosques sombreados y húmedos, cubriendo troncos en descomposición y aferrándose a las rocas, creando mapas fascinantes de colonias.

Moss and Lichen belong to different categories. Moss is a bryophyte, while lichen is a fungus. However, they share a common trait: they are highly sensitive to air pollution. This fact has permitted scientists to use these organisms as indicators of environmental change.

La mousse et le lichen appartiennent à des catégories différentes. La mousse est une bryophyte, tandis que le lichen est un champignon. Cependant, ils ont un trait commun : ils sont très sensibles à la pollution de l'air. Ce fait a permis aux scientifiques d'utiliser ces organismes comme indicateurs des changements environnementaux.

Moos und Flechte gehören zu verschiedenen Kategorien. Moos ist ein Bryophyt, während Flechten als Pilze sind. Sie haben jedoch ein gemeinsames Merkmal: Sie sind sehr empfindlich gegenüber Luftverschmutzung. Diese Tatsache ermöglicht es Wissenschaftlern, diese Organismen als Indikatoren für Umweltveränderungen zu nutzen.

El musgo y el liquen pertenecen a diferentes categorías. El musgo es una briofita, mientras que el liquen es un hongo. Sin embargo, comparten un rasgo común: son muy sensibles a la contaminación atmosférica. Este hecho ha permitido a los científicos usar estos organismos como indicadores de cambio ambiental.

Mosses grow in clumps creating bright green carpets. Some species grow very flat with upward shoots barely rising a few millimeters above the ground, others are a little taller with fern-like shoots.

Moose wachsen in Gruppen und bilden leuchtend grüne Teppiche. Einige Arten wachsen sehr flach mit aufwärts gerichteten Trieben, die kaum wenige Millimeter über den Boden ragen; andere sind etwas höher mit farnartigen Trieben.

Les mousses poussent en touffes pour former des tapis vert vif. Certaines espèces poussent très près du sol avec des pousses ascendantes ne s'élevant qu'à quelques millimètres à peine du sol ; d'autres sont un peu plus hautes avec des pousses ressemblant à des fougères.

Los musgos crecen en grupos creando alfombras de color verde brillante. Algunas especies crecen muy planas con brotes ascendentes que apenas se elevan unos pocos milímetros sobre el suelo; otras son un poco más altas con brotes parecidos a los de los helechos.

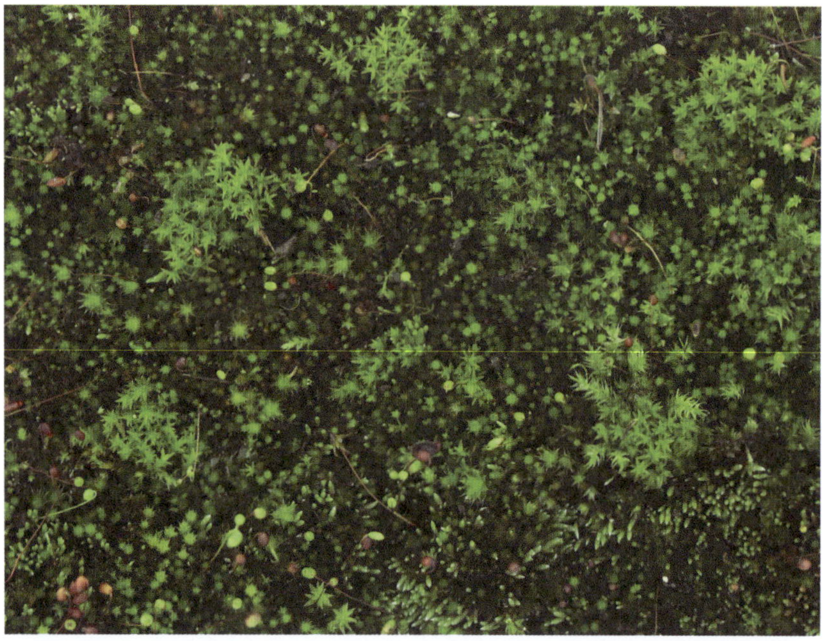

SPROUTING JAR

elaeomyxa

Jannik Wempe has developed a special admiration for tropical landscapes and the rainforest. The creation of terrariums has provided him with a means to surround himself with lush greenery even in the confines of his small student apartment in the city. He is also interested in moss. Over time, he has filled his place with a multitude of small containers with different species of moss and other small plants, creating a personal space that brings him positive vibe and freshness.

Jannik Wempe a développé une admiration particulière pour les paysages tropicaux et la forêt tropicale. La création de terrariums lui a permis de s'entourer de verdure luxuriante, même dans l'enceinte de son petit appartement d'étudiant en ville. Il s'intéresse aussi à la mousse. Au fil du temps, il a rempli son domicile d'une multitude de petits contenants avec différentes espèces de mousse et d'autres petites plantes, créant un espace personnel qui lui apporte une ambiance positive et fraîche.

Jannik Wempe hat eine besondere Bewunderung für tropische Landschaften und den Regenwald entwickelt. Die Einrichtung von Terrarien hat ihm die Möglichkeit gegeben, sich auch auf dem Gebiet seiner kleinen Studentenwohnung in der Stadt mit üppigem Grün zu umgeben. Er interessiert sich auch für Moos. Im Laufe der Zeit hat er seinen Platz mit einer Vielzahl von kleinen Behältern mit verschiedenen Moosarten und anderen kleinen Pflanzen gefüllt und einen persönlichen Raum geschaffen, der ihm positive Stimmung und Frische bringt.

Jannik Wempe ha desarrollado una admiración especial por los paisajes y selva tropicales. La creación de terrarios le ha proporcionado un medio para rodearse de vegetación exuberante, incluso en los confines de su pequeño apartamento de estudiantes en la ciudad. También está interesado en el musgo. Con el tiempo, ha llenado su lugar con una multitud de pequeños contenedores con diferentes especies de musgo y otras plantas pequeñas, creando un espacio personal que le da un ambiente positivo y fresco.

PHOTOS © Jannik Wempe

Jannik keeps a close look at his moss collection to find out under which conditions it will grow best before using it in his terrariums. There is always something new to learn and, in the worse case, he ends up with a pile of desiccated moss.

Jannik wirft einen genauen Blick auf seine Mooskollektion, um herauszufinden, unter welchen Bedingungen sie am besten wächst, bevor sie in seinen Terrarien verwendet wird. Es gibt immer etwas Neues zu lernen und im schlimmsten Fall endet er mit einem Haufen ausgetrocknetem Moos.

Jannik examine de près sa collection de mousses pour savoir dans quelles conditions elle poussera le mieux avant de l'utiliser dans ses terrariums. Il y a toujours quelque chose de nouveau à apprendre et, dans le pire des cas, il se retrouve avec une pile de mousse desséchée.

Jannik observa de cerca su colección de musgo para averiguar en qué condiciones crecerá mejor antes de utilizarlo en sus terrarios. Siempre hay algo nuevo que aprender y, en el peor de los casos, termina con un montón de musgo seco que puede ser útil pare futuros diseños florales.

It is only through close observation and over time that Jannik slowly learns about the morphological diversity of mosses. They are well-suited for the confines of small containers, and even at a small scale, they allow for the creation of versatile looks.

Erst durch genaue Beobachtung und im Laufe der Zeit lernt Jannik langsam die morphologische Vielfalt der Moose kennen. Sie eignen sich gut für den Einsatz in kleinen Behältern, und selbst im kleinen Maßstab lassen sie vielseitige Looks entstehen.

Ce n'est qu'en l'observant de près et au fil du temps que Jannik découvre lentement la diversité morphologique des mousses. Elles sont bien adaptées aux petits contenants et, même à petite échelle, permettent de créer des looks polyvalents.

Es solo a través de la observación cercana y con el tiempo que Jannik aprende lentamente sobre la diversidad morfológica de los musgos. Son ideales para los fondos de pequeños contenedores, e incluso a pequeña escala, permiten la creación de estilos versátiles.

MBOTANIST

mbotanist_

Mbotanist Terrariums was born from Marcus Robinson's desire to capture or mimic an environment he would want to be surrounded by. Inspiration can be found closer than we think. Marcus sources many species of moss from the forest near his home in England. He tries to recreate areas of the forest he has visited inside the capsule of a terrarium. The process might be quite enjoyable and fascinating for some, relaxing and meditative for others.

Mbotanist Terrariums est né du désir de Marcus Robinson de capturer ou d'imiter un environnement dont il voudrait être entouré. L'inspiration peut être trouvée plus près que nous ne le pensons. Marcus trouve de nombreuses espèces de mousses dans la forêt près de chez lui, en Angleterre. Il essaie de recréer des zones de la forêt qu'il a visitées à l'intérieur de la capsule d'un terrarium. Le processus peut être très agréable et fascinant pour certains, relaxant et méditatif pour d'autres.

Mbotanist Terrarien wurde aus Marcus Robinsons Wunsch geboren, eine Umwelt einzufangen oder nachzuahmen, von der er umgeben sein möchte. Inspiration kann näher liegen, als wir denken: Marcus bezieht viele Moosarten aus dem Wald in der Nähe seiner Heimat in England. Er versucht, Bereiche des Waldes, die er besucht hat, in der Kapsel eines Terrariums wiederherzustellen. Der Prozess kann für die einen sehr anregend und faszinierend sein, für die anderen entspannend und meditativ.

Mbotanist Terrariums nació del deseo de Marcus Robinson de capturar o imitar un entorno del que quisiera estar rodeado. La inspiración se encuentra más cerca de lo que pensamos. Marcus obtiene muchas especies de musgo del bosque cerca de su casa en Inglaterra. Intenta recrear dentro de la cápsula de un terrario áreas verdes que ha visitado personalmente. El proceso puede ser muy agradable y fascinante para algunos, relajante y meditativo para otros.

PHOTOS © Marcus Robinson

Plants adopt a different dimension once they are removed from their natural environments and become part of a minute landscape. Tufts of moss become rolling hills and leaves become trees. It's all about scale and size.

Pflanzen nehmen eine andere Dimension an, wenn sie aus ihrer natürlichen Umgebung entfernt werden und Teil einer winzigen Landschaft werden. Moosbüschel werden zu sanften Hügeln und Blätter zu Bäumen. Es geht um Maßstab und Größe.

Les plantes prennent une autre dimension lorsqu'elles sont retirées de leur milieu naturel et s'intègrent dans un paysage minuscule. Les touffes de mousse deviennent des collines ondulantes et les feuilles deviennent des arbres. Tout est une question d'échelle et de taille.

Las plantas adoptan una dimensión diferente una vez que son extraídas de sus ambientes naturales y se convierten en parte de un paisaje diminuto. Los penachos de musgo se convierten en colinas onduladas y las hojas en árboles. Todo es una cuestión de escala y tamaño.

YU-KOKE

www.yukoke.thebase.in   yu.koke.moss

Artistic moss displays in minimalistic transparent glass jars bring lush greenery into interior spaces to satisfy our innate biophilic needs. But beyond this aesthetic quality, moss has lesser-known, yet very important environmental functions. Moss can maintain a consistent level of humidity in a room, both by absorbing and by emitting moisture. Also, it is capable of taking pollutants out of the air, acting as an effective air purifier.

Des présentoirs en mousse artistique dans des bocaux minimalistes en verre transparent apportent de la verdure luxuriante dans les espaces intérieurs pour satisfaire nos besoins biophiles innés. Mais au-delà de cette qualité esthétique, la mousse a des fonctions environnementales moins connues mais très importantes. La mousse peut maintenir un niveau d'humidité constant dans une pièce, à la fois en absorbant et en créant de l'humidité. En outre, elle est capable d'éliminer les polluants de l'air, agissant comme un purificateur d'air efficace.

Künstlerische Moospräsentationen in minimalistischen, transparenten Gläsern bringen üppiges Grün in die Innenräume, um unseren angeborenen biophilen Bedürfnissen gerecht zu werden. Doch über diese ästhetische Qualität hinaus hat das Moos weniger bekannte, aber sehr wichtige Umweltfunktionen. Moos kann ein gleichbleibendes Feuchtigkeitsniveau in einem Raum aufrechterhalten, sowohl durch Aufnahme als auch durch Abgabe von Feuchtigkeit. Auch ist es in der Lage, Schadstoffe aus der Luft zu entfernen und so als effektiver Luftreiniger zu wirken.

Exposiciones artísticas de musgo en frascos de vidrio transparentes y minimalistas que aportan verdor a los espacios interiores para satisfacer nuestras necesidades biofílicas innatas. Pero más allá de esta cualidad estética, el musgo tiene funciones ambientales menos conocidas, pero muy importantes. El musgo puede mantener un nivel constante de humedad en una habitación, tanto absorbiendo como emitiendo humedad. Además, es capaz de eliminar los contaminantes del aire, actuando como un eficaz purificador de aire.

The decorative potential of moss is unquestionable. The world of mosses is rich and diverse. Some mosses come in tufts; others look like miniature pine or palm trees. *Dicranella heteromalla, Mnium hornum, Thuidium tamariscinum, Hylocomium splendens,* and *Rhytidiadelphus squarrosus* are some of the most common species.

Das dekorative Potenzial von Moos ist unbestritten. Die Welt der Moose ist reich und vielfältig. Einige Moose gibt es in Büscheln, andere sehen aus wie Miniaturkiefern oder Palmen. *Dicranella heteromalla, Mnium hornum, Thuidium tamariscinum, Hylocomium splendens* und *Rhytidiadelphus squarrosus* sind einige der häufigsten Arten.

Le potentiel décoratif de la mousse est incontestable. Le monde des mousses est riche et varié. Certaines mousses sont en touffe, d'autres ressemblent à des pins ou de palmiers miniatures. *Dicranella heteromalla, Mnium hornum, Thuidium tamariscinum, Hylocomium splendens* et *Rhytidiadelphus squarrosus* sont parmi les espèces les plus communes.

El potencial decorativo del musgo es incuestionable. El mundo de los musgos es rico y diverso. Algunos musgos vienen en penachos; otros parecen versiones en miniatura de pinos o palmeras. *Dicranella heteromalla, Mnium hornum, Thuidium tamariscinum, Hylocomium splendens* y *Rhytidiadelphus squarrosus* son algunas de las especies más comunes.

Naturalistic displays of moss are enhanced by glass jars, showing the various layers under the pillowy green surface. Mossy landscapes can include other natural materials such as branches and rocks. Gemstones such as fluorite and calcite add a pop of colour and sophistication.

Naturgetreue Moosdarstellungen werden durch Glastiegel ergänzt, die die verschiedenen Schichten unter der kissenförmigen grünen Oberfläche zeigen. Moosige Landschaften können auch andere natürliche Materialien wie Äste und Felsen beinhalten. Edelsteine wie Fluorit und Calcit sorgen für einen Hauch von Farbe und Raffinesse.

L'aspect naturaliste de la mousse est mis en valeur par des bocaux en verre, qui montrent les différentes couches sous la surface verte et coussinée de la mousse. Les paysages de mousse peuvent inclure d'autres matériaux naturels tels que des branches et des rochers. Les pierres précieuses comme la fluorite et la calcite ajoutent une touche de couleur et de sophistication.

Las exhibiciones naturalistas de musgo son realzadas por tarros de vidrio, mostrando las diferentes capas debajo de la superficie verde. Los paisajes musgosos pueden incluir otros materiales naturales como ramas y rocas. Las piedras preciosas como la fluorita y la calcita añaden un toque de color y sofisticación.

MossArt

www.mossart.cn   mossart.cn

MossArt observes moss growing in indoor conditions. A scientific approach fuses with an artistic sensibility to create minute plant worlds. What if one could learn about photosynthesis, respiration and water cycle by tending a terrarium? Growing plants in terrariums, whether open or closed, can teach people about the different natural processes. MossArt specialises in the creation of small plant arrangements, where moss takes centre stage, highlighting the importance of this little known plant for the formation of new environments.

MossArt observe la croissance de la mousse à l'intérieur. Une approche scientifique fusionne avec une sensibilité artistique pour créer des mondes végétaux infimes. Et si l'on pouvait en apprendre davantage sur la photosynthèse, la respiration et le cycle de l'eau en entretenant un terrarium ? Cultiver des plantes dans des terrariums, qu'ils soient ouverts ou fermés, peut enseigner aux gens les différents processus naturels. MossArt est spécialisé dans la création d'arrangements de petites plantes où la mousse occupe une place centrale, soulignant l'importance de cette plante peu connue pour la formation de nouveaux environnements.

MossArt beobachtet, wie Moos unter Innenbedingungen wächst. Ein wissenschaftlicher Ansatz verschmilzt mit einem künstlerischen Feingefühl zu winzigen Pflanzenwelten. Was wäre, wenn man durch die Pflege eines Terrariums etwas über Photosynthese, Atmung und Wasserkreislauf erfahren könnte? Der Anbau von Pflanzen in Terrarien, ob offen oder geschlossen, kann die Menschen über die verschiedenen natürlichen Prozesse informieren. MossArt hat sich auf die Entwicklung von kleinen Pflanzenarrangements spezialisiert, bei denen das Moos im Mittelpunkt steht, und unterstreicht die Bedeutung dieser wenig bekannten Pflanze für die Bildung neuer Lebensräume.

MossArt observa el crecimiento del musgo en condiciones de interior. El enfoque científico se funde con una sensibilidad artística para crear mundos vegetales diminutos. ¿Qué pasaría si uno pudiera aprender sobre la fotosíntesis, la respiración y el ciclo del agua cuidando un terrario? El cultivo de plantas en terrarios, ya sean abiertos o cerrados, puede enseñar a la gente sobre los diferentes procesos naturales. MossArt se especializa en la creación de arreglos de plantas pequeñas, donde el musgo es el protagonista, destacando la importancia de esta planta poco conocida para la formación de nuevos ambientes.

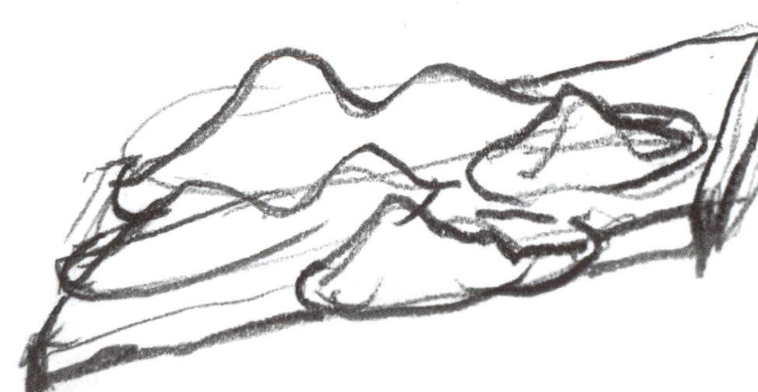

Chinese and Japanese landscape art serve as inspiration for miniature landscapes formed by mounds of soft moss and delicate upright stems evoking the forms and vegetation found in forests, rolling hills, and steep ravines.

L'art paysager chinois et japonais sert d'inspiration à des paysages miniatures formés de monticules de mousse molle et de tiges érigées délicates évoquant les formes et la végétation des forêts, des collines ondulantes et des ravins escarpés.

Chinesische und japanische Landschaftskunst dient als Inspiration für Miniaturlandschaften, die aus Hügeln aus weichem Moos und zarten aufrechten Stängeln bestehen und an die Formen und die Vegetation von Wäldern, sanften Hügeln und steilen Schluchten erinnern.

El arte paisajístico chino y japonés sirve de inspiración para paisajes en miniatura formados por montículos de musgo suave y delicados tallos verticales que evocan las formas y la vegetación que se encuentran en bosques, colinas onduladas y barrancos escarpados.

Moss, natural woods, and other organic features lend to the creation of fantastic wall art. They provide spaces with an inviting feel, add a dramatic natural touch to any interior and, like terrariums, are a creative way to bring the outdoors inside.

Moos, natürliche Hölzer und andere organische Merkmale ermöglichen die Schaffung fantastischer Wandkunst. Sie verleihen Räumen eine einladende Atmosphäre, verleihen jedem Interieur eine dramatische natürliche Note und sind, wie Terrarien, eine kreative Möglichkeit, die natürliche Umgebung in den Innenraum zu bringen.

La mousse, les bois naturels et autres éléments organiques prêtent à la création d'art mural fantastique. Ils donnent aux espaces une atmosphère invitante, ajoutent une touche naturelle dramatique à tous les intérieurs et, comme les terrariums, sont une façon créative d'amener l'environnement naturel à l'intérieur.

El musgo, las maderas naturales y otras materias orgánicas contribuyen a la creación de fantásticas piezas de arte mural. Proporcionan espacios con una sensación acogedora, añaden un toque llamativo y natural a cualquier interior y, al igual que los terrarios, son una forma creativa de traer el entorno natural al interior.

Water gardens are another form of indoor plant display. In this case, the plants are emersed in shallow water, creating a very naturalistic atmosphere. The plants thrive in boggy conditions, have a shallow radicular system and require consistently moist conditions.

Wassergärten sind eine weitere Form der Pflanzenpräsentation im Innenbereich. In diesem Fall werden die Pflanzen in flaches Wasser getaucht, was eine sehr naturalistische Atmosphäre schafft. Die Pflanzen gedeihen unter sumpfigen Bedingungen, haben ein flaches radikuläres System und benötigen konstant feuchte Bedingungen.

Les jardins d'eau sont une autre forme d'exposition de plantes à l'intérieur. Dans ce cas, les plantes sont immergées en eau peu profonde, créant ainsi une atmosphère très naturaliste. Les plantes prospèrent dans des conditions marécageuses, ont un système radiculaire peu profond et ont besoin d'une humidité constante.

Los jardines acuáticos son otra forma de plantas en interior. En este caso, las plantas se sumergen en aguas poco profundas, creando una atmósfera muy naturalista. Las plantas crecen en condiciones pantanosas, tienen un sistema radicular poco profundo y requieren condiciones de humedad constante.

Asian landscape design creates a calming atmosphere, even at a minute scale. Regardless of the size, this calming atmosphere is achieved through a harmonious composition of rocks, plants, and space. The incorporation of Iconic Asian art pieces gives the landscapes a meditative quality.

Asiatische Landschaftsgestaltung schafft eine beruhigende Atmosphäre, auch im kleinsten Maßstab. Unabhängig von der Größe wird diese beruhigende Atmosphäre durch eine harmonische Komposition aus Felsen, Pflanzen und Raum erreicht. Die Einbeziehung von ikonischen asiatischen Kunstwerken verleiht den Landschaften eine meditative Qualität.

L'aménagement paysager asiatique crée une atmosphère apaisante, même à une échelle infime. Quelle que soit sa taille, cette atmosphère apaisante est obtenue grâce à une composition harmonieuse de roches, de plantes et d'espaces. L'incorporation d'œuvres d'art asiatique iconique donne aux paysages une qualité méditative.

Los paisajes asiáticos recrean una atmósfera tranquila, incluso a una escala diminuta. Independientemente del tamaño, esta atmósfera tranquilizadora se logra a través de una composición armoniosa de rocas, plantas y espacio vacío. La incorporación de piezas de arte asiático icónicas otorga a estos paisajes una cualidad meditativa.

MossArt
20190118

TERRALIVING

www.theterraliving.com   terraliving

Founded by a team of passionate scientists and designers with a love for nature, TerraLiving delivers highly customisable terrariums to ensure unique designs adapted to the desires of their buyers. TerraLiving's designs range from portable terrariums like the MossTomo to the sophisticated Titan series. The team uses a great variety of mosses, some commonly used in the creation of terrariums, others rare and therefore, lending to the uniqueness of some designs.

Fondée par une équipe de scientifiques et de designers passionnés et amoureux de la nature, TerraLiving propose des terrariums hautement personnalisables pour assurer des designs uniques adaptés aux désirs de leur clientèle. Les conceptions de TerraLiving vont des terrariums portables comme le MossTomo à la série sophistiquée Titan. L'équipe utilise une grande variété de mousses, certaines couramment utilisées dans la création de terrariums, d'autres rares et donc prêtant à l'unicité de certains dessins.

Gegründet von einem Team leidenschaftlicher Wissenschaftler und Designer mit Liebe zur Natur, liefert TerraLiving hochgradig anpassbare Terrarien, um einzigartige Designs zu gewährleisten, die an die Wünsche ihrer Kunden angepasst sind. Die Designs von TerraLiving reichen von tragbaren Terrarien wie dem MossTomo bis hin zur anspruchsvollen Titan-Serie. Das Team verwendet eine große Auswahl an Moosen, von denen einige häufig bei der Gestaltung von Terrarien verwendet werden, andere selten sind und somit der Einzigartigkeit einiger Designs verleihen.

Fundada por un equipo de científicos y diseñadores apasionados por la naturaleza, TerraLiving ofrece terrarios altamente personalizables para asegurar diseños únicos adaptados a los deseos de sus compradores. Los diseños de TerraLiving van desde terrarios portátiles como el MossTomo hasta la sofisticada serie Titan. El equipo utiliza una gran variedad de musgos, algunos comúnmente utilizados en la creación de terrarios, otros raros y que, por lo tanto, contribuyen a la singularidad de algunos diseños.

Terrariums are a decoration alternative to more usual plant displays such as those mentioned in the previous spread. Plants in terrariums, whether open or closed, definitely last more than cut flowers and just as long as potted plants, provided they are tended adequately.

Verschiedene Moosarten können koexistieren, solange sie auf ähnliche Umweltbedingungen reagieren. TerraLiving hat eine große Auswahl geometrischer Formen entwickelt, um Mini-Landschaften aus verschiedenen Moosarten darzustellen, wobei der Schwerpunkt auf der Subtilität von Farbe und Textur liegt.

Différentes espèces de mousses peuvent coexister tant qu'elles répondent à des conditions environnementales similaires. TerraLiving a conçu une large gamme de formes géométriques pour présenter des mini-paysages formés par différentes espèces de mousses, et qui mettent l'accent sur la subtilité des couleurs et des textures.

Diferentes especies de musgos pueden coexistir siempre y cuando respondan a condiciones ambientales similares. TerraLiving ha diseñado una amplia gama de formas geométricas para mostrar minipaisajes formados por diferentes especies, centrándose en la sutileza del color y la textura.

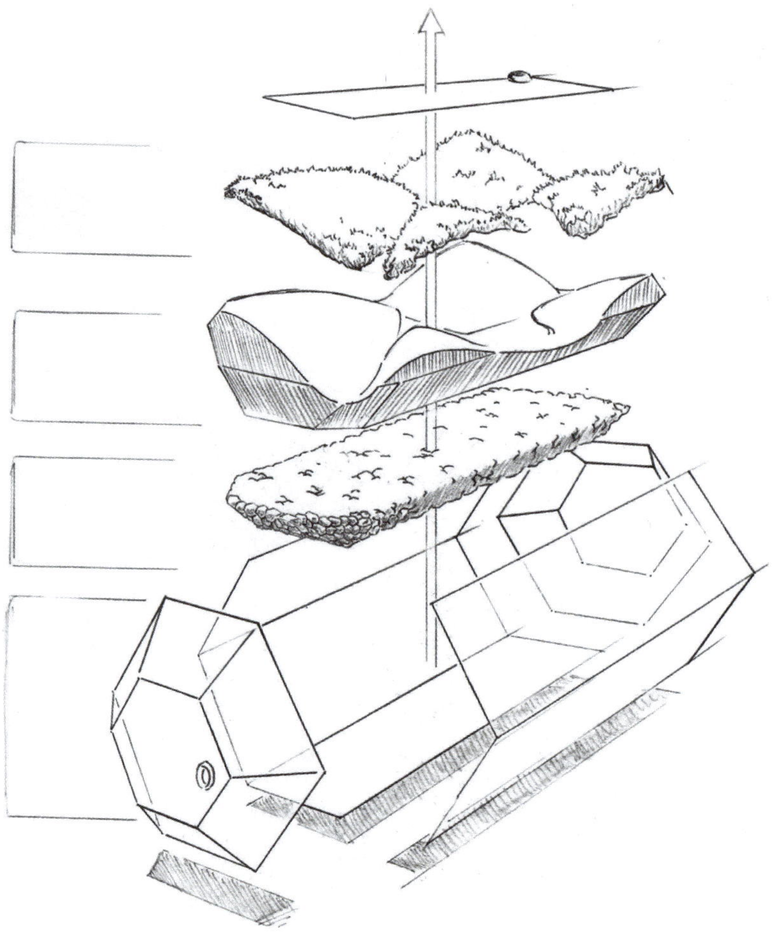

Chronopod
Terra Living

TERRALIVING

YOSHIKO KONDO

yoshiko.kondo

Brya stands for Bryophytes action technology. It is the first successful technology in practical use as maintenance of biological development and indoor purification system. Scientists at Brya have spent over fifty years studying the physiology of bryophytes. The results of the research have reached the point where they can be implemented in various fields in the battle against air pollution paving the way to a healthier living environment.

Brya signifie Bryophytes action technology. Il s'agit de la première technologie réussie dans la pratique pour l'entretien du développement biologique et des systèmes de purification intérieure. Les scientifiques de Brya ont passé plus de cinquante ans à étudier la physiologie des bryophytes. Les résultats de la recherche ont atteint un stade de développement tels qu'ils peuvent être mis en œuvre dans divers domaines de la lutte contre la pollution atmosphérique, ouvrant ainsi la voie à un milieu de vie plus sain.

Brya steht für Bryophytes Action Technology. Es ist die erste erfolgreiche Technologie im praktischen Einsatz zur Erhaltung der biologischen Entwicklung und der Innenreinigung. Die Wissenschaftler von Brya haben über fünfzig Jahre damit verbracht, die Physiologie der Bryophyten zu studieren. Die Forschungsergebnisse sind so weit fortgeschritten, dass sie im Kampf gegen die Luftverschmutzung in verschiedenen Bereichen umgesetzt werden können und den Weg zu einer gesünderen Lebensumwelt ebnen.

Brya significa tecnología de acción de los briofitas. Es la primera tecnología de éxito en su uso práctico como mantenimiento del desarrollo biológico y del sistema de purificación interior. Los científicos de Brya han pasado más de cincuenta años estudiando la fisiología de las plantas briofitas. Los resultados de la investigación han llegado a un punto en el que pueden ser implementados en varios campos en la batalla contra la contaminación del aire, allanando el camino hacia un ambiente más saludable.

Research has proven that mosses are good indicators of air quality. With no root system, moss absorbs water and nutrients through their one-cell-thick leaves. Similarly, they also accumulate and retain air pollutants.

La recherche a prouvé que les mousses sont de bons indicateurs de la qualité de l'air. Sans système racinaire, la mousse absorbe l'eau et les nutriments avec ses feuilles épaisses d'une cellule. De même, elle accumule et retient les polluants atmosphériques.

Die Forschung hat bewiesen, dass Moose gute Indikatoren für die Luftqualität sind. Ohne Wurzelsystem nimmt Moos Wasser und Nährstoffe durch seine einzelligen Blätter auf. In ähnlicher Weise sammeln und speichern sie auch Luftschadstoffe.

Las investigaciones han demostrado que los musgos son buenos indicadores de la calidad del aire. Sin sistema radicular, el musgo absorbe agua y nutrientes a través de sus hojas de un solo gramo de grosor. Del mismo modo, acumulan y retienen contaminantes del aire.

Yukie Ishikawa

bluebell_yuu

So much happens on the forest floor. Nature is spontaneous, producing ephemeral moments. While this can be a challenge for the observer, it does offer the opportunity to seize unique moments. These moments take a whole new dimension when they are captured through a macro lens, witnessing the abundant wonder and radiant beauty of Nature. The images taken reveal intriguing forms, patterns, textures, and subtle colours in a soft light that, most of the time, come unnoticed.

Tant de choses se passent sur le sol de la forêt. La nature est spontanée, produisant des moments éphémères. Bien que cela puisse être un défi pour l'observateur, cela lui offre aussi l'occasion de saisir des moments uniques. Ces moments prennent une toute nouvelle dimension lorsqu'ils sont capturés à travers un objectif macro, témoignant de l'émerveillement abondant et de la beauté radieuse de la nature. Les images prises révèlent des formes, des motifs, des textures et des couleurs intrigantes dans une lumière douce qui, la plupart du temps, passe inaperçue.

Auf dem Waldboden passiert so viel. Die Natur ist spontan und erzeugt flüchtige Momente. Dies kann zwar herausfordernd für den Betrachter sein, bietet aber die Möglichkeit, einzigartige Momente zu erfahren. Diese Momente nehmen eine ganz neue Dimension an, wenn sie durch ein Makroobjektiv aufgenommen werden, welches das reiche Wunder und die strahlende Schönheit der Natur einfängt. Die aufgenommenen Bilder enthüllen faszinierende Formen, Muster, Texturen und subtile Farben in einem weichen Licht, das sonst meist unbemerkt bleibt.

El suelo de un bosque es un lugar de gran actividad. La naturaleza es espontánea, produciendo momentos efímeros. Si bien esto puede ser un desafío para el observador, ofrece la oportunidad de aprovechar momentos únicos. Estos momentos toman una nueva dimensión cuando son capturados a través de una lente macro, presenciando la abundante maravilla y radiante belleza de la naturaleza. Las imágenes tomadas revelan formas intrigantes, patrones, texturas y colores sutiles en una luz suave que, la mayoría de las veces, pasa desapercibida.

No matter where one looks, there is quantity and diversity. There is hardly just one of anything, but rather colonies and clumps of life form in pursuit of survival and replication.

Egal, wohin man schaut, es herrschen Fülle und Vielfalt. Es gibt kaum eines von irgendetwas, sondern Kolonien von geballtem Leben im Streben nach Überleben und Reproduktion.

Peu importe où l'on regarde, il y a de la quantité et de la diversité. Il n'y a pratiquement rien, mais plutôt des colonies et des groupes de formes de vie en quête de survie et de réplication.

No importa dónde se mire, hay cantidad y diversidad; colonias y grupos de formas de vida en busca de la supervivencia y reproducción.

Moss, fungi, lichens, slime mould grow among layers of organic material such as leaves, branches, bark, and stems in various stages of decomposition. However tiny, ephemeral and fragile they might appear, they contribute to the stabilisation of forests ecosystems.

La mousse, les champignons, les lichens, les moisissures visqueuses se développent parmi les couches de matière organique comme les feuilles, les branches, l'écorce et les tiges à divers stades de décomposition. Aussi minuscules, éphémères et fragiles qu'ils puissent paraître, ils contribuent à la stabilisation des écosystèmes forestiers.

Moos, Pilze, Flechten und Schleimpilze wachsen zwischen Schichten aus organischem Material wie Blättern, Zweigen, Rinde und Stängeln in verschiedenen Zersetzungsstadien. So winzig, flüchtig und zerbrechlich sie auch erscheinen mögen, sie tragen zur Stabilität der Waldökosysteme bei.

Musgo, hongos, líquenes y mohos de limo crecen entre capas de material orgánico como hojas, ramas, corteza y tallos en varias etapas de descomposición. Por minúsculos, efímeros y frágiles que puedan parecer, contribuyen a la estabilización de los ecosistemas forestales.

KINOCORIUM

www.kinocorium.net kinocorium

There is an aura of mystery and magic around mushroom terrariums. Mushroom terrariums are not as common as plant terrariums, mainly because there is a greater degree of difficulty in growing mushrooms. The designer of these fantastic fungi worlds emphasises their ephemeral life, which spans no more than a week or two. On the bright side, the process is very exhilarating.

Il y a une aura de mystère et de magie autour des terrariums de champignons. Les terrariums à champignons ne sont pas aussi répandus que les terrariums à plantes, principalement parce qu'il est plus difficile de cultiver des champignons. Le concepteur de ces fantastiques mondes de champignons souligne leur vie éphémère, qui ne dure pas plus d'une semaine ou deux. D'un autre côté, le processus est très exaltant.

Um Pilzterrarien herrscht eine geheimnisvolle und magische Aura. Pilzterrarien sind nicht so verbreitet wie Pflanzenterrarien, vor allem, weil der Pilzanbau schwieriger ist. Der Designer dieser fantastischen Pilzwelten betont ihr flüchtiges Leben, das nicht länger als ein bis zwei Wochen währt. Auf der anderen Seite ist der Prozess sehr berauschend.

Hay un aura de misterio y magia alrededor de los terrarios de hongos. No son tan comunes como los terrarios de plantas, principalmente porque hay un mayor grado de dificultad en su cultivo. El diseñador de estos fantásticos mundos de hongos enfatiza su vida efímera, de una o dos semanas como máximo. Es, sin embargo, un proceso creativo muy estimulante.

PHOTOS © Kazunori Higuchi

Growing mushrooms at home is unlike growing plants. Mushrooms don't need sunlight to grow as plants do, but they don't necessarily need to be in a dark environment either. One thing they do require is a high-humidity environment.

Cultiver des champignons à la maison n'est pas comme cultiver des plantes. Les champignons n'ont pas besoin de la lumière du soleil pour pousser comme les plantes, mais ils n'ont pas nécessairement besoin d'être dans un environnement sombre non plus. Ce qu'ils ont besoin, c'est d'un environnement très humide.

Der Anbau von Pilzen zu Hause ist anders als der Anbau von Pflanzen. Pilze brauchen kein Sonnenlicht, um zu wachsen wie Pflanzen, aber sie müssen sich auch nicht unbedingt in einer dunklen Umgebung befinden. Etwas, das sie benötigen, ist eine Umgebung mit hoher Luftfeuchtigkeit.

El cultivo de hongos en casa no es como el de las plantas. Los hongos no necesitan la luz del sol para crecer, pero tampoco necesitan de un espacio oscuro. Sí necesitan, sin embargo, un ambiente muy húmedo.

MOSSLIGHT-LED

https://mosslight-led.amebaownd.com/ mosslight1955

Blown glass vessels with integrated LED light ensure plants survival and growth even in dark rooms while providing interior spaces with some greenery. Illuminated, the plants seem as lively as if they were bathed by sunlight after a rainfall. LED lighting has advanced to the point that its spectral intensity can be customised to suit the different stages of plant growth. Gone are the days when greenhouse gardeners used high-pressure sodium or fluorescent lamps, which presented various functional and environmental disadvantages.

Les récipients en verre soufflé avec lumière LED intégrée assurent la survie et la croissance des plantes, même dans les pièces sombres, tout en donnant un peu de verdure aux espaces intérieurs. Illuminées, les plantes semblent aussi vivantes que si elles étaient baignées par la lumière du soleil après la pluie. L'éclairage LED a progressé au point que son intensité spectrale peut être personnalisée pour s'adapter aux différents stades de croissance des plantes. Fini le temps où les jardiniers de serre utilisaient des lampes au sodium haute pression ou fluorescentes qui présentaient divers inconvénients fonctionnels et environnementaux.

Geblasene Glasgefäße mit integriertem LED-Licht sichern das Überleben und Wachstum der Pflanzen auch in dunklen Räumen und geben den Innenräumen etwas Grün. Beleuchtet wirken die Pflanzen so lebendig, als würden sie nach einem Regenfall vom Sonnenlicht gebadet. Die LED-Beleuchtung ist so weit fortgeschritten, dass ihre spektrale Intensität an die verschiedenen Phasen des Pflanzenwachstums angepasst werden kann. Vorbei sind die Zeiten, in denen Gewächshausgärtner Natriumdampf-Hochdruck- oder Leuchtstofflampen verwendeten, die verschiedene funktionale und ökologische Nachteile aufwiesen.

Los recipientes de vidrio soplado con luz LED integrada aseguran la supervivencia y el crecimiento de las plantas incluso en habitaciones oscuras, al mismo tiempo que proporcionan a los espacios interiores algo de verdor. Iluminadas, las plantas parecen tan vivas como si estuvieran bañadas por la luz del sol después de una lluvia. La iluminación LED ha avanzado hasta el punto de que su intensidad espectral puede personalizarse para adaptarse a las diferentes etapas del crecimiento de las plantas. Atrás quedaron los días en que los jardineros de invernadero utilizaban lámparas de sodio o fluorescentes de alta presión, lo que presentaba varias desventajas funcionales y ambientales.

PHOTOS © Nobuaki Uchino

Moss provides enchanting scenery, carpeting rock and log surfaces with cushy, vivid green patterns. Mosses are bryophytes, the most primitive of land plants. They barely rise a few centimetres above the ground, but these minute plants play a crucial role in regulating ecosystems.

Moos bietet bezaubernde Landschaften, Teppiche auf Fels- und Holzoberflächen mit gemütlichen, leuchtend grünen Mustern. Moose sind Bryophyten, die primitivste aller Landpflanzen. Sie erheben sich nur wenige Zentimeter über den Boden, aber diese winzigen Pflanzen spielen eine entscheidende Rolle bei der Regulierung von Ökosystemen.

La mousse offre des paysages enchanteurs, de la moquette, de la roche et des surfaces en rondins avec des motifs vert vif et pépère. Les mousses sont des bryophytes, la plus primitive des plantes terrestres. Elles s'élèvent à peine à quelques centimètres du sol, mais ces minuscules plantes jouent un rôle crucial dans la régulation des écosystèmes.

Moss ofrece paisajes encantadores, alfombras de roca y superficies de troncos con patrones de color verde vivo y suave. Los musgos son *briofitas*, las plantas terrestres más primitivas. Apenas se elevan unos pocos centímetros por encima del suelo, pero estas diminutas plantas desempeñan un papel crucial en la regulación de los ecosistemas.

Moss has made its way to terrarium design, provoking bewilderment and awakening curiosity among terrarium artists and plant lovers. Their intriguing rarity is an invitation to learn more about the world of bryophytes.

Moos hat seinen Weg in die Terrariengestaltung gefunden, was bei Terrarienkünstlern und Pflanzenliebhabern Verwirrung und Neugierde weckt. Ihre faszinierende Seltenheit ist eine Einladung, mehr über die Welt der Bryophyten zu erfahren.

La mousse a fait son chemin vers la conception de terrariums, provoquant la perplexité et éveillant la curiosité des artistes de terrarium et des amateurs de plantes. Leur rareté intrigante est une invitation à en apprendre davantage sur le monde des bryophytes.

El musgo ha hecho su camino hacia el diseño de terrarios, despertando la curiosidad entre los artistas de terrarios y los amantes de las plantas. Su intrigante rareza es una invitación a aprender más sobre el mundo de los *briofitas*.

Mosslight-LED functions as a light source and a decorative portable greenhouse, all in one. Because Mosslight-LED has integrated lighting that promotes growth, its placement is not limited to be near a window with good light.

Mosslight-LED fungiert als Lichtquelle und dekoratives, tragbares Gewächshaus in einem. Da Mosslight-LED über eine integrierte Beleuchtung verfügt, die das Wachstum fördert, ist die Platzierung nicht auf einen Fensterplatz mit gutem Licht beschränkt.

Mosslight-LED fonctionne comme une source de lumière et une serre portable décorative, tout-en-un. Parce que Mosslight-LED a intégré un éclairage qui favorise la croissance, il n'est pas nécessaire de la placer près d'une fenêtre avec une bonne lumière.

El Mosslight-LED funciona como una fuente de luz y un invernadero decorativo portátil, todo en uno. Debido a que Mosslight-LED tiene iluminación integrada que promueve el crecimiento, su colocación no está condicionada a estar cerca de una ventana con buena luz.

BAIOSPHERE

www.baiosphere.de   baiosphere

Baiosphere is a table lamp that combines design and nature. Its versatile design suits any decor and any space, whether it's the office or the bedroom. The integrated full-spectrum LED are conceived to mimic natural sunlight, helping the mini landscape contained in the transparent container grow healthy. The landscape forms an almost self-sustaining biotope, bringing a piece of calming nature.

Baiosphere est une lampe de table qui allie design et nature. Son design polyvalent s'adapte à tous les décors et à tous les espaces, qu'il s'agisse du bureau ou de la chambre à coucher. Les LED à spectre complet intégrées sont conçues pour imiter la lumière naturelle du soleil, aidant le mini paysage contenu dans le conteneur transparent à se développer sainement. Le paysage forme un biotope presque autosuffisant, apportant un morceau de nature apaisante.

Baiosphere ist eine Tischleuchte, die Design und Natur vereint. Ihr vielseitiges Design passt zu jeder Einrichtung und jedem Raum, ob im Büro oder im Schlafzimmer. Die integrierten Vollspektrum-LEDs sind so konzipiert, dass sie das natürliche Sonnenlicht nachahmen und die im transparenten Behälter enthaltene Miniaturlandschaft gesund halten. Die Landschaft bildet ein fast selbsttragendes Biotop und bringt ein Stück beruhigende Natur.

Baiosphere es una lámpara de mesa que combina diseño y naturaleza. Su diseño versátil se adapta a cualquier decoración y a cualquier espacio, ya sea la oficina o el dormitorio. Los LED de espectro completo integrados están concebidos para imitar la luz solar natural, ayudando a que el mini paisaje contenido en el envase transparente crezca sano. El paisaje forma un biotopo casi autosuficiente, aportando un trozo de naturaleza tranquilizadora.

Baiosphere can contain a variety of ecosystems, ranging from a tropical forest to an arid desert. It is completely sealed to maintain the environmental stability required for the survival and growth of the plants.

La Baiosphere peut contenir une variété d'écosystèmes, allant d'une forêt tropicale à un désert aride. L'écosystème est complètement scellé pour maintenir la stabilité environnementale nécessaire à la survie et à la croissance des plantes.

Die Baiosphäre kann eine Vielzahl von Ökosystemen enthalten, die von einem tropischen Wald bis zu einer trockenen Wüste reichen. Sie ist vollständig versiegelt, um die für das Überleben und Wachstum der Pflanzen erforderliche Umweltstabilität zu gewährleisten.

La Baiosphere puede contener una variedad de ecosistemas, desde un bosque tropical hasta un desierto árido. Está completamente sellada para mantener la estabilidad ambiental necesaria para la supervivencia y el crecimiento de las plantas.

VON
HALLERS
GIN

VON UND ÜBER

The functional design can be seen as a portable laboratory allowing for observation while bringing a decorative touch to any interior space.

Le design fonctionnel peut être considéré comme un laboratoire portable permettant d'observer tout en apportant une touche décorative à tout espace intérieur.

Das funktionale Design kann als tragbares Labor betrachtet werden, das eine Beobachtung ermöglicht und gleichzeitig jedem Raum eine dekorative Note verleiht.

El diseño funcional se puede ver como un laboratorio portátil que permite la observación y aporta un toque decorativo a cualquier espacio interior.

LEGROW

kinocorium legrow.winmartdesign

LeGrow offers unique modular designs for year-round indoor mini gardens. Each individual pot is a building block. The pots can be arranged horizontally and vertically, creating forms adapted to the user's needs. The system includes planting pots, LED grow lamps, humidifiers, and a special pot with four USB charging ports. Altogether, the components allow for unique arrangements fusing technology and Nature.

LeGrow offre des conceptions modulaires uniques pour des mini jardins intérieurs toute l'année. Chaque pot individuel est un élément constitutif. Les pots peuvent être disposés horizontalement ou verticalement, créant des formes adaptées aux besoins de l'utilisateur. Le système comprend des pots de plantation, des lampes de culture LED, des humidificateurs et un pot spécial avec quatre ports de charge USB. Dans l'ensemble, les composants permettent des arrangements uniques qui fusionnent la technologie et la nature.

LeGrow bietet einzigartige modulare Designs für ganzjährige Indoor-Minigärten. Jeder einzelne Topf ist ein Baustein. Die Töpfe können horizontal und vertikal angeordnet werden, so dass Formen entstehen, die den Bedürfnissen des Benutzers angepasst sind. Das System umfasst Pflanztöpfe, LED-Pflanzenlampen, Befeuchter und einen speziellen Topf mit vier USB-Ladeanschlüssen. Insgesamt ermöglichen die Komponenten eine einzigartige Kombination aus Technologie und Natur.

LeGrow ofrece diseños modulares únicos para mini jardines interiores durante todo el año. Cada maceta individual es un bloque de construcción que se puede colocar horizontal o verticalmente, creando formas adaptadas a las necesidades del usuario. El sistema incluye macetas, lámparas de crecimiento LED, humidificadores y una maceta especial con cuatro puertos de carga USB. En conjunto, los componentes permiten arreglos únicos que fusionan la tecnología y la naturaleza.

LeGrow

LeGrow

eGrow
LeGrow

LeGrow Shine is a combination of various pots and LED lamps. The light is height adjustable and is perfect for winter growing. Technology advances offer a wide variety of energy-efficient lamps to replace their massive and power-guzzling predecessors such as the high-pressure sodium lights.

LeGrow Shine ist eine Kombination aus verschiedenen Töpfen und LED-Lampen. Die Leuchte ist höhenverstellbar und eignet sich hervorragend für den Winteranbau. Der technologische Fortschritt bietet eine Vielzahl von energieeffizienten Lampen, die ihre massiven und stromfressenden Vorgänger wie die Natriumhochdrucklampen ersetzen.

LeGrow Shine est une combinaison de différents pots et lampes LED. La lumière est réglable en hauteur et est parfaite pour la culture hivernale. Les progrès technologiques offrent une grande variété de lampes éconergétiques pour remplacer leurs prédécesseurs massifs et énergivores, comme les lampes au sodium haute pression.

LeGrow Shine es una combinación de varias macetas y lámparas LED. La luz es regulable en altura y es perfecta para el cultivo en invierno. Los avances tecnológicos ofrecen una amplia variedad de lámparas de bajo consumo para reemplazar a sus predecesoras, las lámparas de sodio de alta presión, que consumían mucha energía.

LeGrow

The LeGrow Spring set includes a humidifier in addition to a number of pots. This system is aimed at improving indoor air quality. Not only does this system provide moisture to grow plants, but it has also shown to have health benefits for people.

Le set de ressorts LeGrow comprend un humidificateur en plus d'un certain nombre de pots. Ce système vise à améliorer la qualité de l'air intérieur. Non seulement ce système fournit de l'humidité pour faire pousser des plantes mais il se révèle aussi bénéfique pour notre santé.

Das LeGrow Spring Set beinhaltet neben einer Reihe von Töpfen auch einen Luftbefeuchter. Dieses System zielt auf die Verbesserung der Raumluftqualität ab. Es spendet nicht nur Feuchtigkeit für den Pflanzenanbau, sondern bietet nachweislich auch gesundheitliche Vorteile für den Menschen.

El juego LeGrow Spring incluye un humidificador además de varias macetas. Este sistema tiene por objeto mejorar la calidad del aire interior, proporcionando no solo humedad para el crecimiento de las plantas, sino que también ha demostrado tener beneficios para la salud.

LeGrow planters have integrated water reservoirs, which capture the excess of water preventing spills. This system also minimises the need for watering in favour or a low maintenance and water saving system. The Quick Charging Pot with four USB ports is ideal for workspaces.

Die LeGrow-Pflanzgefäße verfügen über integrierte Wasserbehälter, die den Überschuss an Wasser aufnehmen und so ein Verschütten verhindern. Dieses System minimiert auch den Bedarf an Bewässerung zugunsten oder ein wartungsarmes und wassersparendes System. Der Schnellladetopf mit vier USB-Anschlüssen ist ideal für den Arbeitsplatz.

Les jardinières LeGrow sont équipées de réservoirs d'eau intégrés qui captent l'excès d'eau et préviennent les déversements. Ce système minimise également le besoin d'arrosage en faveur d'un système d'entretien et d'économie d'eau à faible maintenance. Le pot de chargement rapide avec quatre ports USB est idéal pour les espaces de travail.

Las sembradoras LeGrow tienen depósitos de agua integrados que captan el exceso de agua evitando derrames. Este sistema también minimiza la necesidad de riego a favor de un sistema de bajo mantenimiento y ahorro de agua. El cargador rápido con cuatro puertos USB es ideal para espacios de trabajo.

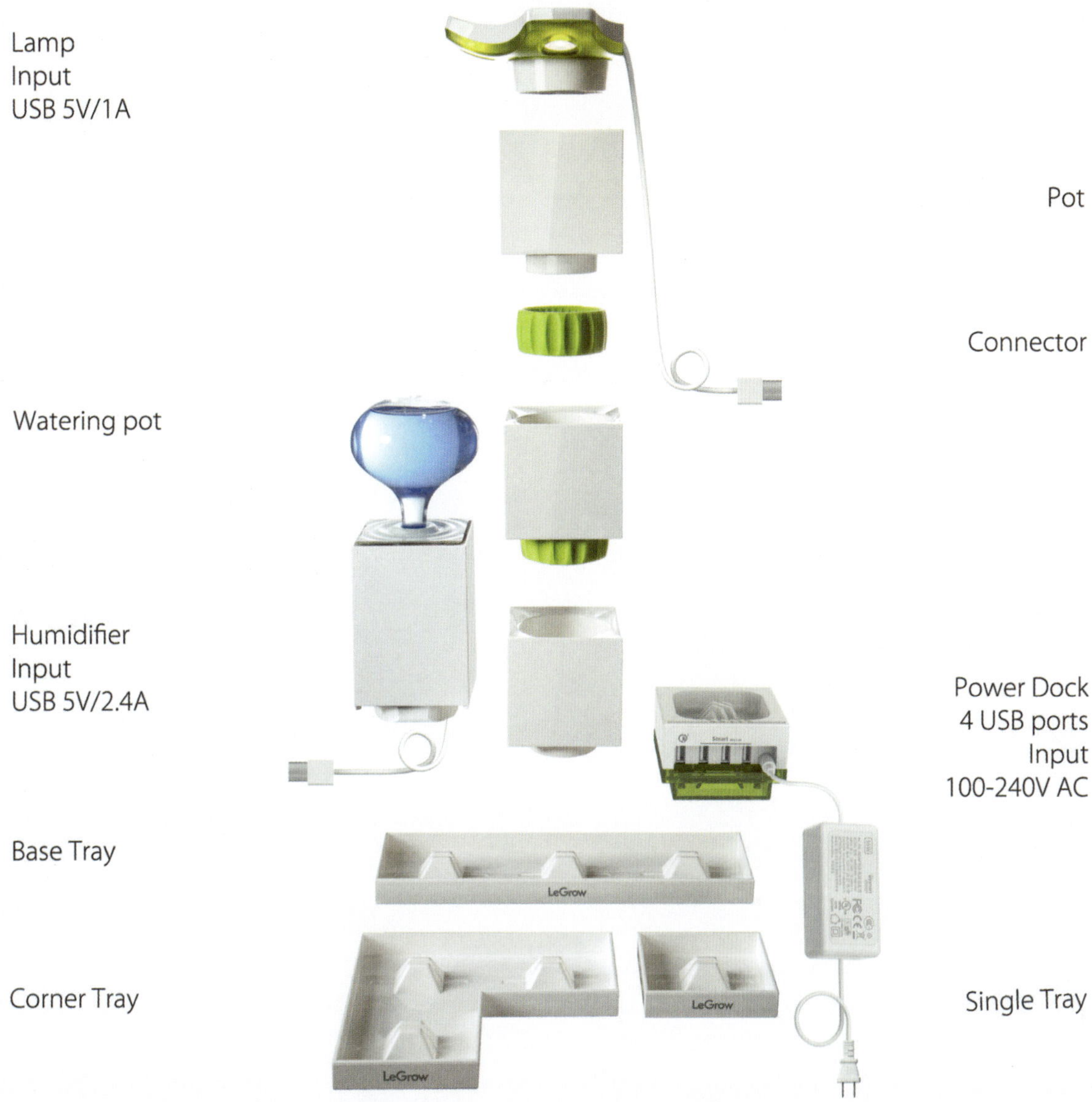
Lamp
Input
USB 5V/1A
Pot
Connector
Watering pot
Humidifier
Input
USB 5V/2.4A
Power Dock
4 USB ports
Input
100-240V AC
Base Tray
Corner Tray
Single Tray
LeGrow